MW01144644

THE NEW "N" WORD

The White Middle Class

WHAT OTHERS HAVE TO SAY....

"Jim Hill's clarion call for the middle class to wake up to what is happening to them and to vote to turn the tide for a brighter future couldn't be more timely and comes from unique life experiences. From his childhood in a single mother household in Atlanta, Georgia, to his life in public service, Jim brings wisdom, warmth and empathy to his tale of what is happening to middle class America who are victims of greed, a corrupted campaign finance system and seemingly unbridled corporate power. He gives the reader hope as he lays out an agenda of policies that will return the country to the one he first fell in love with years ago. Jim has a love of country and firm belief that Americans – if they vote – will reject the politics of hate and greed permeating the country."

Chuck Sheketoff, public policy analyst and advocate

"I first met Jim Hill when he was running for State Representative. Jim Hill was an easy candidate to support. He was principled, respectful of differing opinions while holding strong unwavering beliefs of his own, and committed to making a difference in other people's lives. You get to know someone when you work on their campaign for office and they win; but, you **REALLY** get to know someone when they lose. I learned that Jim Hill is a really good man. That Jim Hill is principled just as much after a loss as he was in the hope of success. That Jim Hill's commitment to making a positive difference in the lives of other people comes from the depths of his soul. Jim Hill's greatest strength is his deep compassion for other people. It does not surprise me at all that he would write a book dedicated to improving the lives of working class Americans."

Gary Bruebaker, former Oregon Deputy State Treasurer

THE NEW "N" WORD

The White Middle Class

BY

JIM HILL

PORTLAND • OREGON
INKWATERPRESS.COM

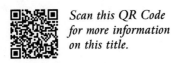

*Scan this QR Code
for more information
on this title.*

Copyright © 2016 by Jim Hill

Cover and interior design by Masha Shubin
Author photos by Jim Meuchel

All rights reserved. No part of this book may be reproduced or transmitted in any form or by any means whatsoever, including photocopying, recording or by any information storage and retrieval system, without written permission from the publisher and/or author. The views and opinions expressed in this book are those of the author(s) and do not necessarily reflect those of the publisher, and the publisher hereby disclaims any responsibility for them. Neither is the publisher responsible for the content or accuracy of the information provided in this document. Contact Inkwater Press at inkwater. com. 503.968.6777

Hill, Jim, 1947- author.
    The new "N" word : the white middle class / by Jim
Hill.
        pages cm
        Includes bibliographical references.
        LCCN 2016903196
        ISBN 978-1-62901-350-3 (pbk.)
        ISBN 978-1-62901-351-0 (Kindle)

        1. Middle class whites--United States--Economic
conditions--21st century. 2. Hill, Jim, 1947-
3. Lawyers--Biography. 4. Legislators--Oregon--Biography.
5. United States--Politics and government--21st century.
6. Autobiographies. I. Title.

HT690.U6H55 2016   305.5'50973
                        QBI16-600044

Publisher: Inkwater Press | www.inkwaterpress.com
Paperback ISBN-13 978-1-62901-350-3 | ISBN-10 1-62901-350-1
Kindle   ISBN-13 978-1-62901-351-0 | ISBN-10 1-62901-351-X

Printed in the U.S.A.

3 5 7 9 10 8 6 4 2

"What the United States does tells the difference of right and wrong to the world."

Nelson Mandela, 1994

To my Mother, for her unwavering support for me to write this book.

Also to Dennis, Becky, Steve, Steve S., Floyd, Lisa, Deb, and Jack, for their persistent interest and encouragement. And in memory of Big Al. My deepest appreciation to the staff of the Oregon Supreme Court Library—not only for their hospitality but also for their genuine friendship. Also, special thanks for the courtesy shown me by the Oregon State Police Officers who kept us safe. Finally, my deepest gratitude and affection to my dear friend and manager, Mari Anne, without whom this book would not have been possible.

CONTENTS

"A nation of sheep eventually gets fleeced by its government."

Jim Hill

CITIZENS FOR TAX FAIRNESS ↓

PER CAPITA PERSONAL INCOME — COMPARED TO
OTHER COUNTRIES?

— COMPARED TO OTHER TIMES?

p17 WHAT DOES IT MEAN FOR re COST OF LIVING.
A CORPORATION TO
HAVE "OFFSHORE" (NON-TAXED) IN THE LONG RUN, ITS NO DIF. THAN
PROFITS? INCOME AVERAGING, ONCE THEY REPATRIATE THE OFFSHORE PROFITS

COMPARE CORPORATE PROFITS VS CORPORATE TAXES

p18 VS TIME

p32 COMPARE AVE EXECUTIVE PAY VS WORKERS
(373X MORE)
IN 2014

p40 COMPARE BANK ASSETS OF
10 LARGEST BANKS
TO ALL THE REST — DOES IT EXCEED 77%?

FORMS OF WORLD DOMINATION
MILITARY
ECONOMIC,
'CYBER'IC

DID CHINA SUPPORT DARFUR GENOCIDE?
SYRIAN

p44 DID IT TAKE 9 YEARS TO GET CONGRESS TO
MEDICALLY HELP 9/11 FIRST RESPONDERS?
DID THE BILL ACTUALLY HELP?

p46 WHAT'S A 'PAYROLL TAX MORATORIUM'?

p50 WHAT WERE THE RULES (THAT WERE REPEALED) ABOUT
MEDIA OWNERSHIP?

p51 WHAT DOES MURDOCH'S 'NEWS CORP'
SAY ABOUT GLOBAL CLIMATE CHANGE?

'DAILY MAIL'
NEWS OF THE WORLD'

WHAT OTHER MEDIA
DOES MURDOCH CONTROL?

p53 HOW IS POLITICS DESCRIBED?

p59 ELIGIBLE VOTER TURN-OUT ~36.3%

p61 HOW DID JUDGES DECIDE TO WEAKEN VOTING RIGHTS
ACT OF 65 IN 2013?

p63 TRACK THE RATE OF INCOME GROWTH OF THE TOP 1%

WHAT % HAVE FULL TIME JOBS ?   44% IN 2013
P64 WAS THE BAILOUT $700 B. ?
    ✓ AMERICANS FOR TAX FAIRNESS
    ✓ U.S. DEPT. OF TREASURY re JOBS RECOVERED
                                    SINCE 2008
P24 ✓ CORELOGIC re HOME VALUE
                    UPS/DOWNS
            re HOUSEHOLD WEALTH

WHY IT IS IMPORTANT FOR AMERICA TO BE #1

P37 ✓. CURRENT EFFORTS re GLASS-STEAGALL
P41   (WAS REPEALED IN 1999)
173   WHY ? WHAT ?
                                 WAS THE LOGIC,
                                 WAS IT INTERNA-
                                        TIONAL ?

I T'S OFFICIAL: WE'RE NUMBER TWO. FOR THE FIRST TIME IN MODERN history, the American middle class is no longer the wealthiest middle class in the world.

That's right, our neighbors to the north, the Canadians, have surpassed us. Their per capita personal income is now higher than ours. After decades of increasing prosperity and upward mobility in the standard of living for middle-class America, why are we now stagnating while our northern friends continue to prosper? The reason is that their government still believes in serving all of its people, while ours now allows the American middle class to be exploited and abused by the super-rich and powerful. This is not only bad news for the majority of Americans; it is detrimental to the well-being and future of our great country. The so-called "developing countries" point with pride to the growth of their middle classes as the best evidence of their progress toward economic growth and prosperity. But the simple fact is that our middle class is being gutted, and as a result, the potential of our country is being held back. The only thing worse is that we are standing by like a bunch of suckers

✓ ON WRITINGS BY JANE MAYER re KOCH BROS.
   (NEW YORKER)
                OR
            FRANK RICH
            (N.Y. TIMES)

and chumps, allowing it to happen even though we have all of the power to stop it.

This is not about cheerleading and pandering to your sense of patriotism. This is about how important American values are to the world, and what the world would be like if the United States was not the most powerful nation on earth. Imagine the world without our military greatness. After World War II, the entire world would now be living under brutal tyranny. Imagine the world without our economic greatness. The standard of living for us and so many around the world would be far less. Imagine the world without our scientific and medical achievements.

But most importantly, imagine what the world would be like without the greatness of our belief in freedom and democracy for all people. It is true that we are far from perfect and we do not always live up to the principles that our country was founded upon. I know that personally, as an African American who grew up in the South under the laws of racial segregation. Nevertheless, the world is a far better place because of our influence. It needs us to continue to be that way if more and more of the world's people are to finally enjoy freedom and justice.

Imagine the world where the dominant influence is China or Russia. While many of their people are making economic gains, if they challenge the will of the government they go to prison or worse. If these governments treat their own people that way, how do you think they would treat the rest of us? To illustrate this point, consider what occurred in Corvallis, Oregon, in the summer of 2012. Chinese officials who were visiting the city noticed a mural on a building; the mural advocated freedom for Tibet. The officials went to the mayor of Corvallis and insisted that she force the owner to remove the mural from the building. She, of course, declined. This was a very small incident as far as international diplomacy is concerned; however, it is a true indication of the attitude of the Chinese towards the rest of the world. Ask the people of Tibet, Darfur, and Hong Kong.

The point is that we still live in a world of aggression, whether it is military or economic. There must be a country in this world that is willing and able to stand up against tyranny and injustice. Whether we like it or not, that country is ours. We are the only nation that is strong enough militarily and economically to force down any aggressor. With great power comes great responsibility. As Nelson Mandela said, "What the United States does tells the difference of right and wrong to the world."

So the real question is not whether or not the United States is the most powerful nation in the world, but whether we will remain so. There are those who say that America will go the way of previous "empires" that have risen to greatness, and then decayed and fell apart. They say that our leadership and influence in the world is on an inevitable decline that will continue until we are a second-rate power, overtaken by China and other nations. They say that we have lost the competitive edge and spirit that made us great, and that we are only resting on past accomplishments while the rest of the world is gaining on us and will eventually surpass us.

But our decline is not inevitable, because the greatness of America is based on the freedom and opportunity that it provides for its people. As long as Americans are free and our government serves us by investing in all of our talent, skill, and potential, there is no reason we cannot become greater and greater forever. There are no outside forces–whether hostile nations, terrorists, or anything else—capable of taking this country down. The only way that the United States will decline is if we forget the principles of freedom, fairness, and opportunity that are our foundation, and begin to rot from the inside. It is the responsibility of each of us to see that this never happens.

Our Constitution puts all the power in the peoples' hands to make this country whatever we want it to be.

In order for the United States to have the most influence in the world, it has to continue to have the strongest economy. When we stand by and allow Wall Street bankers to be vampires that suck the life out of our economy, we are complicit in taking our great nation down. It is obvious that they don't care how much they hurt the country, as long as they get super-rich. If they did care, they wouldn't keep doing the things that brought the United States economy to its knees and damaged the lives of so many of their fellow Americans. This is truly incomprehensible selfishness, greed, and conceit, and it must be stopped. Are you a Great American? Will you vote out of office the politicians who are allowing these giant banks to continue to have their way? Will you at least vote?

This small book is dedicated to the belief that all Americans will come to remember and appreciate how blessed we are to live in a country where we are free; where the power of our government belongs to us and truly is of the people, by the people, and for the people.

However, with this privilege of being an American comes the responsibility to hold our government officials accountable. We must insist that they live up to the principles of our Constitution by serving all of the people equally, fairly, and in a way that gives each of us a genuine opportunity to make a better life for ourselves and thereby assure our country's greatness. This is what made our country great and this is what is necessary to keep it so.

Right now, our country is struggling. We can blame that on anyone we want, but ultimately We the People are responsible, because we have all of the power. Each of us has a role in getting our country back on the path of greatness and the American Dream for all Americans. Will you stand up and be a Great

American? You don't have to be rich, famous, or powerful. You don't have to belong to any group, organization, or political party. All that it takes is for each of us to care about this wonderful country enough to vote!

UNWAVERING FAITH IN THE AMERICAN DREAM

[handwritten annotation: THE AMERICAN DREAM IS 2 PARTS: 1) AMERICA'S PRINCIPLES (VS SHORT-COMINGS) 2) AMERICANS' ECONOMIC OPPORTUNITIES NOW VS PAST]

I WAS BORN IN 1947 IN ATLANTA, GEORGIA, WHICH MEANS THAT I grew up when racial discrimination was the law. The systematic, pervasive degradation of black people taught me what injustice was. Even in grade school, when we recited the Pledge of Allegiance and got to "and liberty and justice for all," I understood that those words were not meant for us. I simply knew that the way we were being treated was wrong, because it was unfair. Perhaps it was then that I developed the desire to do what I could to make sure that no American would be treated the way we were.

Time and again, it was the government—particularly the federal government—that stood up against the bigotry and racism in the south so that we could gain our full Americanhood. For that reason, I felt drawn to public service.

After graduation from law school, my first job was with the Oregon Department of Justice. It was a wonderful experience. My main responsibility was to see that criminal convictions obtained at the trial level were upheld in the appellate courts. However, because the Attorney General's office was the state's lawyer on all legal matters, there were opportunities to be involved in all types of cases. The common denominator was that, directly or indirectly, we argued for what was in the best interest for Oregon and its people. Even though we didn't make as much money as lawyers in the private sector, I had the opportunity to work with and learn about government from some of the best attorneys in the state.

After a few years, I began to realize that I wanted to be one of the people who actually made the laws. I remembered how it felt when Congress passed the Civil Rights Act in 1964 and the Voting Rights Act in 1965, under the incredible determination and leadership of President Lyndon Johnson, a southerner.

I finally summoned the courage to run for state representative in 1980. I lost that election by sixty-one votes. I lost for a number of reasons. I was outspent three to one. It was the year of the Reagan sweep. I was a Democrat while my district was the second-most-Republican in the state, and predominantly white. President Carter conceded defeat before the polls closed on the West Coast. The House Democratic Office reneged on the help they promised me. I later found out that they were polling in my race. The poll said that I was gaining fast, but the House Democratic leadership didn't believe it, though they believed the same poll for other candidates. They obviously found it hard to believe that an African American could poll high in such a white conservative district. They never shared any poll results with me, which of course would have been very helpful and encouraging. However, the main reason that I lost was that I just didn't do enough door-to-door canvassing. We had an old district map that completely left out a new precinct. Even though I lost, that election dispelled the notion that the people of Salem, Oregon were too prejudiced to vote for a black candidate. I formed a bond with the people that I will always cherish. Two years later, I ran again. We learned from our mistakes, and I won by a landslide.

At that time, Oregon was in a deep recession. Our main industry, timber, lost many thousands of well-paying family-wage jobs, as high interest rates crippled the housing industry nationwide. Many Oregonians were truly suffering. We were desperate to revitalize our economy. Economic Development became my primary issue and remained so throughout my political career. In 1984 I was re-elected. At the same time, the people voted to create the Oregon lottery, with its proceeds dedicated to economic development. I was appointed to be the House Co-Chair of the Joint Committee on Trade and Economic Development, which was assigned the task of effectively using the lottery's proceeds to stimulate our economy. Over time, Oregon made a comeback as we diversified the economy and made the state part of the high-tech "Silicon Forest" of the Pacific Northwest. It was impossible to conceive that twenty years later, our economy would again be brought to its knees by an even worse recession, due to the greed and irresponsibility of the big Wall Street banks.

I was elected state senator in 1986. I was one of the primary leaders to pass a number of bills that enacted the "Anti-Apartheid Act," made Martin Luther King's birthday a state holiday, and added sexual orientation to the list of crimes under Oregon's Harassment law. In 1992, I was elected State Treasurer, becoming the first person of color elected to statewide office in Oregon. My excellent staff and I doubled the pension fund from $20 to $40 billion dollars, improved the state's bond rating, and set up a venture capital fund that allocated lottery proceeds to finance Oregon businesses and create jobs. We also led an effort to promote financial literacy.

When I was State Treasurer, I had the honor and privilege of meeting Nelson Mandela in South Africa after the fall of apartheid.

I presented a token of appreciation to him in 1994, expressing our thanks for giving us hope, and especially for those of us who thirst for freedom, justice, and opportunity. He thanked America for helping to fight against poverty and for a better life.

The greatness of this man, as with all truly great leaders, was his desire and ability to bring his people together after his country had been torn apart by what seemed to be insurmountable divisiveness. I could tell he cared about all of his people, white and black. He was about fairness, justice, and opportunity for all. He did not seek retribution and vengeance against those who had inflicted ultimate injustice and suffering upon black South Africans, and who had imprisoned him for over twenty years. This was in shameful contrast to our own country, where some of our own so-called leaders seek to repress and take away opportunity from the majority of Americans by doing the bidding of the mean-spirited super-rich and powerful, whose sole motivation is selfishness and greed. In America, we are blessed that we don't have to fight and die for our freedom. All we have to do is vote for leaders who understand the simple notion that the greatness of our country is based on the fairness and opportunity for all of us that is called the American Dream.

One of the great things about getting older is the sense of perspective you develop about your life's journey. Experiences from your past become even clearer than when you were actually living them. In the context of the American Dream, a black kid like me, who grew up in Georgia, was elected to the state legislature, then to statewide office, in a state that is predominantly white. My journey (and that of so many other Americans) was much harder than it should have been, because some people believed that they were entitled to deprive us of our Americanhood. If it weren't for the extraordinary strength and sacrifice of my mother, I would not have had my opportunity to live a piece of the Dream. My mother remembers how the Ku Klux Klan burned a cross on my grandparent's front yard, simply because they bought and owned the extremely modest home that they lived in. Ownership of property, the Klan believed, was only for white people. Yet their grandson got a real chance at the American Dream.

There was a time in my life when I felt that a revolution was the only way for black people to have freedom and fairness—the only way to respond to the unrelenting bigotry and hatred of people who made it clear that they were willing to do absolutely anything to keep us down. But people like Dr. King and especially my mother convinced me that one day the Dream would be for us too, because this is America. They were right. My family's journey (and that of so many others) is a testament that the American Dream is coming true. However, it is not guaranteed to any of us. It seems that there will always be elitists, who believe that only they are entitled to it. Today, the entire American middle class—who is, of course, mostly white people—is being stripped of the Dream by discrimination based on class, wealth, and power. When was the last time that you got a raise? The sad truth is that over the last forty years the income of the entire middle class has declined.

THE NEW "N" WORD—THE WHITE MIDDLE CLASS

IRST, MY MOST SINCERE APOLOGY FOR USING THE "N" WORD. OBVIously, it is the one of the most offensive and controversial words in our language—not only for African Americans, but also for anyone who abhors the harshest demeaning of another human being.

But having said that, imagine my shock at what is happening today. You probably ask "How can the middle class be an "n" word when most of middle class America is white?" The "n" word is much more than a description of skin color. It is an attitude that says that you are innately inferior to me, and therefore I have the right to mistreat and use you any way that I please. I know this attitude very well, having grown up in the South. People declared themselves superior to us simply because their skin was white. Every facet of life was cast in terms of race and designed to oppress and demean us in every way possible. Even though my mother protected me from the worst aspects of this racism and taught me that the only one that I had to bow down to was God, the experiences of those times are still with me.

I hope you understand my utter shock and dismay to see, in

the context of present-day America, white people treated like we African-Americans were back in the South. While this discrimination is not as violent or as obvious, it is just as real. If you are middle class, you are being decimated—and it is not being done by Obama or any of us minorities. It's being done by a bunch of greedy white men on Wall Street, and is being done to you by another bunch of greedy, super-rich, power-hungry white men who care as little about you as they do about us. In this book I call them "plutocrats": people whose power derives from their wealth.

All of the middle class (and those who aspire to be in the middle class) are being discriminated against, regardless of background. However, make no mistake about it—most of the victims of this discrimination are white people, especially white men, because white people make up the vast majority of the American middle class and have been the biggest losers of middle class wealth. Specifically, it is discrimination based on economic status.

Look at the facts. Who lost the most wealth when the bloated, incompetent banks on Wall Street almost caused a depression? Who lost most of the millions of jobs? Who owned most of the millions of businesses that went bankrupt? Who owned most of the millions of homes that were and are being foreclosed upon? Whose schoolchildren are now getting inferior educations because of the thousands of teachers laid off due to budget cuts? Whose are most of the college students that are now over a trillion dollars in debt because there were no jobs for them when they graduated? Whose income has been flatlining for at least the last forty years? The answer to all these questions: mostly white people. The middle class is suffering a death of a thousand cuts.

This was once the kind of treatment reserved for black people. The new "n" word thesis does not mean that old-fashioned racism is no longer an issue. It is. But now we are seeing a new type of discrimination against the middle class, in favor of some of the super-rich, who believe that their wealth makes them better than the rest of us. Their attitude: why go to the trouble of getting elected to government when we can just buy it and not be accountable to anyone? Unfortunately, many of the people that we elected to Congress agree with them. They hide behind the term "conservative" and use it as an excuse to be mean and do the bidding of those who regard the rest of us as serfs, whose only purpose is to serve them and make them richer. In turn, they get all of the cash that they need for their political campaigns.

During my eighteen years as an elected official, I served with true conservatives. The terms "liberal" or "conservative" were not nearly as important as an individual's integrity, sense of fairness, and (most of all) commitment to the people of Oregon. If these qualities were present, we almost always found common ground, and did what was best for the state and its people. Regardless of party affiliation or political philosophy, none of us exhibited disdain toward the people who chose us to represent them. Unfortunately, those days have given way to a new level of partisan bickering where integrity takes a back seat to the Party.

As the bumper stickers used to say, "Mean People Suck." There is no excuse for the kind of behavior we see today. We honor politicians by electing them to public office, and then they turn around and slap us in the face. This kind of treatment is why we had the American Revolution. In America, there are no kings and queens, and people are not entitled simply because they are wealthy. As our Declaration of Independence states: "We hold these truths to be self-evident, that all men [and women] are created equal, that they are endowed by the

Creator with certain unalienable rights, that among these are life, liberty, and the pursuit of happiness."

To the King of England, we were subjects, not equals. Some of the super-rich and powerful in this country, including some of the elected people we have hired, view us the same way. This is the old concerted effort to make us feel that somehow we are not worthy of the American Dream, instead of acknowledging that without the rest of us, they would have nothing. This is why I say that the middle class, especially the white middle class, is the new "n" word. Do you think that slave owners were grateful to the slaves for making them rich? Of course not. They pushed them down even harder. Once some people plant it in their twisted minds that they are innately superior to you and you are innately inferior to them, things like freedom and fairness become meaningless. To them, what you think or feel simply doesn't matter. To them, you are nobody. Like slaves, you are made to feel inferior for making them rich. All mean people suck, but mean people with a lot of money can do some serious damage to the rest of us.

It is time for us to remind these elitists who and what this country is all about. Who has fought and died for this country and saved us from being conquered and enslaved? The super-rich? No. Some of them just make a lot of money from war. There is a lot of money being made in Iraq and Afghanistan, for instance—but it is not being made by our soldiers, who deserve it. No wonder that Dick Cheney was so adamant about invading Iraq, even though there were no weapons of mass destruction. His company, Halliburton (where he used to be the CEO), made a fortune from that war. Ever notice how warmongers like Cheney have never served in the military? Yet they are perfectly willing to sacrifice American sons and daughters even if the premise of the war is based on a lie. Again, there is that attitude of privilege and entitlement, even when lives are at stake.

One of the latest "big lies" that the powerful are trying to perpetrate is that half of all Americans are a bunch of tax-dodging moochers who would rather get government handouts than work. They point out that half of us pay no taxes. Of course, what they forget to mention is that the porkers on Wall Street destroyed the economy and killed millions of jobs and businesses. This is the old classic trick of blaming and demeaning the victims, while nothing happens to the greedy, incompetent bandits who stole our livelihoods and got richer doing it. All that anyone has to do is look at this country and the highest standard of living that we used to enjoy to know that Americans are some of the hardest working people in the world. The truth of the matter is that it is hard to pay taxes when your job or business has been snatched away from you.

Furthermore, the hypocrisy of these plutocrats has no bounds. While they berate the jobless for not paying taxes, many of the largest, richest corporations and individuals in America pay little or no income taxes at all. *Mother Jones*, a non-profit dedicated to investigative reporting, stated that, "While the rest of us sweat out our taxes, 2/3 of U.S. Corporations pay no federal income tax."[1]

According to a 2013 Report by *Americans for Tax Fairness,*

- Citigroup had $42.6 billion in profits offshore in 2012 on which it paid no US taxes.[2] Citigroup would owe $11.5 billion in US taxes if profits were brought home. (This is one of the worst of the banks that caused the financial crisis in the US and had to be bailed out with billions of our tax dollars.)

- General Electric made $88 billion from 2002–2012 and paid just 2.4 percent in taxes for a tax subsidy of $29 billion. They paid no taxes i.e., in four years out of that period. GE had $108 billion in profits offshore in 2012, on which it paid no US taxes. They received $21.8 billion in federal contracts from 2006–2012. GE also eliminated more than 15,000 American jobs since 2004, while adding 30,000 jobs overseas during that time.

- FedEx made $6 billion over the last three years and didn't pay a dime in federal income taxes.

- ExxonMobil paid just a 15 percent federal income tax rate from 2010–2012. That's less than half the official 35 percent corporate tax rate—a tax subsidy of $6.2 billion. Exxon-Mobil had $43 billion in profits offshore in 2012, on which it paid no US taxes.

According to the report, "Corporate profits are at a 60-year high, while corporate taxes are near a 60-year low." Furthermore, "in 1952, under Republican President Dwight D. Eisenhower, corporate income taxes were nearly a third of the federal government's receipts but had declined to less than 10 percent by 2012. This is due to a corporate tax code riddled with loopholes, perks and preferences." The offshore tax loophole costs the US Treasury $90 billion a year.

Corporations avoid taxes by spending hundreds of millions of dollars to hire lobbyists to contribute hundreds of millions of dollars to Congressional campaigns; politicians in turn are more than willing to provide these corporations with whatever tax loopholes they want. The corporate giants and some of the super-rich individuals say that they are only doing what the law allows. Of course, what they fail to mention is that it is they who are really determining what the law is. What a deal! The result is that those of us who are not rich enough to buy and take advantage of these loopholes get to carry most of the tax burden. Again, it is the middle and upper-middle class that is paying. If you are not at least a multimillionaire several times over you cannot belong to the tax-free club; mere millionaires and high "thousandaires" need not apply. So pay up, suckers.

The purpose of our government, according to the United States Constitution, is to serve all of the people and the country. The embodiment of this service is our military. They embrace the word and the ideal of service to country. They proudly say that they are (or were) "in the service." It is interesting that our country's truest patriots, who put their minds, bodies, and lives on the line for us, are comfortable with the idea of service, while many of the people we elect to public office actually treat us and the country with disdain and disrespect. They lord it over us, ignore us, and even hurt us as if they are some kind of ruling class and we are their servants who have to take whatever mistreatment they dish out.

This has got to stop. It is hurting our country and us. The simple fact is that our government is being sold by our elected officials, and is being bought out from under us by some with an ocean of money. These plutocrats believe that their money makes them better than the rest of us, as if they were some kind of royalty. As was said in George Orwell's book, *Animal Farm*, "All animals are equal, but some are more equal than others."[3]

I have no doubt that most of us have a deep, abiding love for our country. However, I believe that we have forgotten and take for granted how fortunate we are to live in a country where we are free. I fear that we have become so jaded and spoiled about our freedom and the American Dream that we have forgotten that it can be taken from us if we allow it. That is what is happening to us right now, and we are submitting to it as if we are helpless victims instead of the ones who have all the power.

We control the executive branch of our government because we elect our president. We control the legislative branch because we elect our senators and representatives. We control the judicial branch because the senators that we elect must confirm the judges. In many states, we elect our state and local judges, prosecutors and law enforcement officials directly. In a capital murder case, the people, in the form of the jury, have the ultimate power of deciding whether an individual lives or dies (in states with the death penalty). Nowhere in the world do people have more freedom from their government and more power over it. Do we no longer appreciate and cherish that our government was founded to serve us—instead of control, dominate, abuse, and even murder us (as some tyrants are doing to their people, today)?

Unfortunately, for most people in the world, we are by far the exception rather than the rule. Look at what has been happening since the Arab Spring in the Middle East and North Africa. There was an unexpected, spontaneous uprising by people demanding their freedom. They were not soldiers; nor were they insurgents who wanted only money, power, and vengeance. They were mostly unarmed. Yet they were fearless. They were willing to suffer and die. They were saying what we said when our country was born—"give us liberty or give us death"—and like us, they meant it.

What is the response of their so-called leaders? They are shooting their own people down in the streets. These tyrants are actually firing artillery and calling it airstrikes on innocent men, women, and children. This repression and murder has been going on for years, yet they are not backing down. My Fellow Americans (hereafter, "MFA"), many people around the world have to make the ultimate sacrifice for just a chance at what we already have.

Oppressed people look to America as the shining example of what their lives could be. We must never take our freedom for granted. We don't have to die for it because so many Americans have already done that—and continue to do that—for us. All of the power of our government is already in our hands. Perhaps more than any time in our country's history, we need to exercise it. Our failure to exercise our power has created a vacuum that is being filled by people and organizations with oceans of money. They are more than willing to spend that money to make our government of them, by them, and for them, only. To them, the rest of us don't matter, we are just something to be used up and discarded. When are we going to stand up to these would-be dictators, and remind them that this is our country, too, by voting their flunky politicians out of office? ARE YOU A GREAT AMERICAN?

WHAT AMERICAN DREAM?

INCREDIBLY, ACCORDING TO THE 2010 CENSUS, ONE IN TWO AMERIcans live below the poverty line or have earnings that classify them as low income! MFA, we are the richest nation on earth. There is no way that half of us should be living anywhere near the poverty line, unless something in our country has gone terribly wrong. More than half of those who live below the poverty line are our children.

Here are a few of the ways in which our country is particularly suffering at the moment.

EMPLOYMENT: Since[4] the financial crisis began in 2008, we have lost over 8.8 million jobs, according to the US Department of Treasury in April 2012. It will take years for us to recover.

HOUSING: Our housing market has all but collapsed. Millions and millions of Americans have lost their homes to foreclosure since 2008, and the number is still rising. *Corelogic* reported in 2013 that there were 4.4 million foreclosures during this time

WE CAN'T JUST EDUCATE OURSELVES INTO NON JOBS!

JOB OPPORTUNITIES W/ OUT THE POST GRAD TRAINING (THE POST GRAD EDUCATION) DOESN'T EXIST.

NOT SO SURE — W/ OUT HOME TO CLOSE TO REAL (THE REAL EDUCATION)

and more are being filed each day.[5] Ninety percent of American homes have declined in value, the highest number on record.

HOUSEHOLD WEALTH LOST: According to the same US Department of Treasury report referenced above, $19.2 trillion was lost in household wealth since the financial crisis.[6]

OLDER AMERICANS: Millions of Americans who have worked hard, saved, and invested all of their lives for a decent retirement, have lost that money when they need it most. This is not about deadbeats. This is about millions of middle-class Americans who have worked hard, saved, invested, and done everything that should be done to have a piece of the American Dream. This is about people who have worked to give their children an opportunity for a better life, only to face the prospect that their children are likely to be worse off than they are. Because of severe cuts to state and local budgets, the most vulnerable people in our society are facing reduction or elimination of truly vital services and programs.

EDUCATION: Education is the great equalizer in our country. It epitomizes our belief in (and commitment to) equal opportunity and fairness for all. It is the main factor giving each American a chance for a better life, regardless of background. It is the main catalyst for the talent and skills of our people, and it helps make our country the greatest.

If we are to maintain our standing in the world and keep the American Dream alive, our government must invest our tax dollars in us, the people, by providing the best education and training in the world. If our educational system declines, our country will decline. It really is that simple. Education is an investment, not an expense.

Most of us are aware that the "Greatest Generation" (parents of the baby boomers) literally saved the world for democracy and freedom by winning World War II. However, right after the war, they also went on to make the United States the strongest peacetime economy in the world. The main factor that allowed them to accomplish this was the G.I. Bill, passed by Congress, which invested in the training and education of our returning soldiers. It paid for college and all kinds of education and training opportunities that helped us make the transition from a wartime economy. The standard of living that we enjoy today is founded on the investment that was made in the American people due to this piece of legislation.

Perhaps we don't realize how important something is unless we are deprived of it. As an African -American who grew up under racial segregation in the South, where we were deemed inferior by law, I knew without a doubt how important a good education was to our struggle for freedom and equality. My mother taught me—and other parents taught their children— that if a white person had a grade school education, we had to have a high school diploma. If they had a high school diploma, we had to have a college diploma. If they had a college diploma, we had to have a master's degree. If they had their masters, we needed a PhD to be considered equally intelligent and educated. During slavery, why do you think it was against the law to teach a slave how to read? The slave owners knew that knowledge was power, and that if they could keep us ignorant, they had a better chance of keeping us powerless.

The American system of education used to be the envy of the world. Now, country after country is surpassing us. If this continues, they will surpass us in other ways, including economically and militarily. Imagine what might have happened at the end of World War II if our technological and scientific superiority had not produced the atomic bomb. It is estimated that it would have cost the lives of hundreds of thousands of American soldiers if we had invaded Japan. It was our technological, scientific, and economic superiority that eventually ended the Cold War, too. The former Soviet Union simply could not keep up with us. The same advantages enabled us to put men on the moon and to bring them back safely. There is an old saying that is truer today than ever. A nation has no power without brainpower.

So what is happening to the American educational system that used to be the best? For our youngest Americans, we are closing schools and laying off large numbers of classroom teachers for the first time in decades. During my political career, I can't tell you how many times I heard phrases such as "our children are our most important asset" or "our children are our future" or something similar. Like so many things that we used to stand for in this country, words like these are becoming empty platitudes.

Along with many in my generation, I am a grandparent. The experience is as wonderful as everybody says it is. But I cannot help but focus on the future and the kind of country and world that we are passing on to these precious young people. The truth is that regardless of how much we say we love our children, if we don't demand that our federal government help our beleaguered state and local governments provide them with the best education possible, we are failing them and literally undermining the future of our country.

It is not just our youngest students that are being short-changed educationally. Our economic near-collapse has caused tuition at our colleges, universities, and other post-high school educational institutions to rise to the point of being prohibitive for too many young people and their parents. They have been forced to take on a lifetime of student-loan debt that they cannot repay because of the crippled job market. MFA, this debt is over one trillion dollars. When these loans become due and cannot be repaid, not only will there be dire consequences for students and their parents, but also for the whole country, especially if there has to be another bailout similar to that caused by the financial mortgage crisis.

The worst part about all of this is that it didn't have to happen at all. It was caused by a small group of rich, powerful, greedy, incompetent men, who wanted to get richer at all costs, no matter how many lives they damaged, or how much they hurt their country—and, indeed, the entire world—in the process.

THE MODERN-DAY ROBBER BARONS

A T THE OUTSET, I WANT TO MAKE IT CLEAR THAT I HAVE NO PROBLEM at all with people being rich or super-rich, nor do I in any way object to the great concentrations of wealth in our businesses, corporations, or individuals. Indeed, such wealth is necessary if we are to effectively compete in this global economy. But most importantly, in America, it is wrong to discriminate against anyone on the basis of how much money they have or don't have. I state this because there are those in the media and politics that start squealing and yammering about "class warfare" any time the issue of economic discrimination is raised, even if the allegations are supported by the facts. By the way, if there is class warfare, it is the middle class that is definitely losing. As Warren Buffet—one of the wealthiest men in America—said, "There's class warfare, all right, but it's my class, the rich class, that's making war, and we're winning." For the American middle class, wage growth has all but stopped. In real terms, wages have actually declined—a trend that has been going on for decades.

I strongly believe in our system of free enterprise. My first real job was at age thirteen. I was an errand boy for Citizens

Trust Company—then located on Auburn Avenue, in Atlanta. This was the first black-owned full-service commercial bank in the country. One day, my mother told me that we were going to the bank. When we got there, instead of going to one of the tellers, we went and sat in the waiting area of the CEO, Mr. L. D. Milton. When I asked my mother why we were there, she just told me to be patient. When Mr. Milton invited us in, he asked us to sit down. Without wasting any time, my mother asked, "Will you give my son a job?" Mr. Milton looked at me, then replied, "But what can he do?"

I was not prepared for her answer. "You don't have to pay him," she said. "I just want to keep him off of the streets." Her boldness paid off. Mr. Milton hired me to do odd jobs around the bank. They did pay me a small amount of spending money every week, and at the end of the summer, they gave me a stipend to help my mother pay for my boarding school tuition at St. Emma Military Academy in Virginia.

I worked at Citizens Trust Company every summer until I graduated. It was a valuable introduction to the world of business and free enterprise. However, my most cherished experience there was meeting Dr. Martin Luther King. He came into the bank on a fairly regular basis. One day I was there; I immediately recognized him. My supervisor saw me staring, and asked if I would like to meet him. I was terrified, but of course I did. We went up to him and my supervisor introduced me. I was so intimidated that I could barely speak. Dr. King stuck out his hand and I shook it. I will never forget his smile and his kindness. On subsequent visits he acknowledged me whenever he saw me. These experiences grow more and more valuable to me each year when we celebrate his day.

While our system of free enterprise may not be perfect, history has shown that it is the best way to allocate scarce natural and financial resources. It has enabled the United States

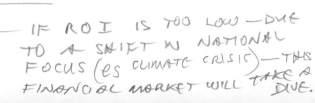
IF ROI IS TOO LOW —DUE TO A SHIFT IN NATIONAL FOCUS (es CLIMATE CRISIS)—THIS FINANCIAL MARKET WILL TAKE A DIVE.

to become the richest and most powerful nation in the world. That is why the rest of the world imitates us, including "communist" China. Wall Street is vital to the well-being of our country because it is supposed to be the main allocator of financial resources. Investments should be made in the most meritorious businesses based on which of them earn (or could earn) the highest returns on the money invested. One way or another, Wall Street touches just about all of our lives.

When I was State Treasurer of Oregon, my duties as the state's chief financial officer gave me the opportunity to become familiar with Wall Street and some of the best financial minds in the world. I felt fortunate and privileged to have an excellent staff and the opportunity to learn about and participate in our free enterprise system at its highest levels. By prudently investing our government employees' retirement dollars, we not only grew the pension fund to secure their retirements, but we also knew that our investments were playing a role in strengthening our state and national economies, and that they produced jobs. In that scenario, everybody won. That is American free enterprise at its best. If we keep this system fair, strong, and honest, the economic future of our country is unlimited.

The Wall Street that I knew was a meritocracy where the rules of free enterprise were based on the cornerstone of fair competition. If you were good at what you did and played by the rules, you succeeded. If not, you failed, and there was always someone trying to do it better. The system had integrity. I did not think it was possible that a few unprofessional, greedy, irresponsible egomaniacs could or would bring it to its knees.

There have been a number of books and TV programs about the details of the 2008 financial crisis. To summarize, the CEOs of the largest and most powerful financial institutions in the world bankrupted their companies by selling toxic investments to investors here and around the world, sending the US economy and, indeed, the economy of most of the world to the very brink of collapse. Actually, it is being extremely charitable to say that they sold "investments." In truth, they were no more than get-rich-quick schemes that violated any notion of the "prudent person investment rule". Then they put a gun to the head of our government and said, "We are too big to fail—so you have to give us hundreds of billions of taxpayer dollars or there will be a worldwide depression. Oh, and by the way, we are going to use *your* taxpayer dollars to pretend that we were profitable and give ourselves the largest salaries and bonuses in our history." This was nothing but blatant and gross corporate welfare. The Associated Press (AP), reporting in June of 2008, wrote that

> as the US economy slowed to a crawl and stockholders watched their money evaporate, CEO pay still chugged to yet more dizzying heights last year . . . Collectively, the 10 best-paid CEOs made more than half a billion dollars last year. Yet half the members of this stratospheric club were leading companies whose profits shrank dramatically . . . Rick Wagoner, chief executive of General Motors Corp., announced earlier this month the company had to close four plants that make trucks and SUVs because of lagging demand as fuel prices soared. That followed the posting of a $39 billion loss in 2007, a year when its stock price fell by about 19 percent without adjusting for dividends. And Wagoner? His pay rose 64 percent to $15.7 million.[7]

That same year, Lloyd Blankfein, CEO of Goldman Sachs Group, took in $53 million, while the head of Morgan Stanley, B. John Mack, took in a paltry $41.7 million in pay, perks, and stock options combined. The newest numbers show that the pattern hasn't changed: the average executive was paid 373 times more than workers in 2014. When was the last time you got a meaningful raise?

The only thing that is more outrageous than what the banks did is that our so-called government has allowed them to get away with it. However, the saddest part of all of this is that we, the people, have allowed our government to let the banks hurt us so badly and get away with it.

The bankers' message is crystal clear. *We can destroy the economy; cause you to lose millions of jobs, homes, businesses, and pensions; take your tax money; and shatter your lives. Then we are going to give ourselves the fattest rewards ever for doing it. We can do any damn thing we want to you, this country, and even the world—and there is nothing you can do about it, because we own the government and the people you elected to supposedly serve you.*

There is no limit to the arrogance and sense of entitlement of these people. According to *Time*, after the federal bailout of $182 billion of our tax dollars for American International Group (A.I.G.)—the insurance company whose failure threatened to bring down much of the global financial system— the former A.I.G. CEO billionaire Hank Greenberg had the nerve to turn around and sue the federal government for billions of dollars, alleging that the bailout hurt his company's shareholders. As *Time* writer Michael Grunwald wrote, "So we should mock the gall of the litigants who are suing the fire department that saved their homes. Still, we can recognize that some of their furniture got wet."[8] The *New York Times* reported in June 2015 that Judge Thomas C. Wheeler of the United States Court of Federal Claims handed down a split decision. "Yes, he ruled, the Fed had indeed crossed the legal line by demanding a 79.9 percent equity stake in A.I.G. as a condition of the bailout in 2008. But at the same time, the government was also correct that

A.I.G. shareholders had not been damaged; in fact, they had been saved from bankruptcy and certain doom. He declined to award any damages."[9]

SUCKERS AND CHUMPS

AVE WE BECOME A NATION OF SUCKERS AND CHUMPS THAT JUST LIES down and takes this kind of abuse? If we allow this to go unpunished and unfixed, allowing the possibility that it could happen again, then that is exactly what we are, and we deserve everything we are getting now and when it happens again in the future. The stock market used to be a place where a prospering American middle class could invest in order to increase our wealth, maintain a good standard of living, and prepare for a decent retirement. Now, we are no longer prospering. Indeed, we are getting poorer. The outrageous irresponsibility of these bankers destroyed trillions of dollars of middle-class wealth. Even if we had money to invest, most of us were burned so badly that we have lost all confidence in the fairness and integrity of the market. We fear that it could all happen again. We must face the fact that these big banks now own our Congress, both parties. Even after the financial carnage of the last few years, our elected officials stand with them against us. How long are we going to stand by and let them rob us of the American Dream? The American Dream is about every American having a real opportunity to make more money—not just a bunch of smug, super-rich elitists who think the dream is only for them. We must stand up for our Americanhood and vote these people out.

These people are drunk with power and money. They have no concept of the idea that with great power comes great responsibility. They act as if they are kings who reign over the rest of us with impunity. They don't even have respect for the interests of the people that they have a fiduciary duty to. In many instances they took actions that benefited themselves at the expense of their clients and shareholders.

Since the financial crisis began in 2008, the six largest US banks, led by J.P. Morgan Chase (the supposed best-run of the group) and Bank of America, have incurred more than $100 billion in legal fees in the process of litigating and settling claims arising from their misconduct. That is more than all of the dividends paid to their shareholders between 2008 and 2012. It is more than their combined profits for 2012. And there is more to come.

Even after they laid waste to the lives of so many people, they are completely unrepentant. They spend hundreds of millions of dollars hiring lobbyists and making political contributions to our (actually their) senators and representatives in both parties, blocking every effort at reform. They want to keep doing exactly what they were doing when they caused this debacle, as if it never happened. MFA, they hired 3,000 lobbyists—five lobbyists for every senator and representative.

They want to continue to drive ninety mph through school zones and residential neighborhoods. They don't care who gets hurt, as long as they get richer and the rest of us have to pay for the damage. Why should they care? They can't lose. They believe that they have enough money and power to force us to bail them out again, no matter how badly they foul things up. When they need it, they just roll out the victim card. In January

2015, Jamie Dimon, CEO of JP Morgan Chase said that "big banks are under attack." Really? They have been allowed to get away with all but destroying the economy and ruining people's livelihoods, and he's whining about being "under attack"? There is no limit to the arrogance and insensitivity of these people.

I have tried to imagine what would have happened to me if, when I was State Treasurer of Oregon, I had run the state's finances so deeply into the ground that the taxpayers had to bail me out—and then turned to them and demanded a raise. I would have been running for my life, and I would've deserved to be caught. In truth, if I had done to my state's finances what these bankers did to their companies' (and our nation's) finances, I would have resigned in shame. But not these guys, because they have no shame, no honor, and no conscience. If you asked any other CEO—from Fortune 500 companies on down—what would have happened if they did to their companies what these CEOs did to their banks, they would tell you the same thing. If they didn't resign first, they would have been fired in disgrace.

Also, I try to imagine how the press and media would have treated me for destroying the state's finances and demanding a raise. They would have burned my bones to ashes—and deservedly so. But when it came to the Wall Street disaster, the financial press and media was almost silent about who was responsible. If the financial media had spent half as much time holding these bankers accountable as they do worshipping and kissing up to them, this near-depression could have been avoided.

Incredibly, even after the financial meltdown caused by these giant banks, some in the financial media and their commentators continue to whine that they are overregulated. They must have been unconscious since 2008. These bankers bought all of the deregulation that political cash could buy—including their holy grail of deregulation, the repeal of Glass-Steagall, the law that has protected us from this kind of financial catastrophe for over 70 years since the Great Depression. They got all of the freedom and power they could want. Then they horrifically abused it. The financial media is so bedazzled by these corrupt bankers that they have forgotten a basic rule of society. If you abuse your freedom or your power, it will be taken from you. If a few people like them didn't abuse their freedom and power, we would hardly need any laws or regulations at all. After the financial destruction that they caused, calling for more deregulation is like calling for less law enforcement in the face of a crime wave.

The financial media is constantly portraying themselves as advocates and defenders of free enterprise. Apparently, they don't really understand what free enterprise is. What these Wall Street bankers did is not free enterprise. What they did is a perversion of free enterprise. The fact is that they are some of the worst CEOs in the history of American free enterprise because of the staggering amounts of money that they lost for their companies and shareholders. If it were not for our tax dollars, their banks would be broke and in bankruptcy. Yet they continue to act as if they are royalty. The reality is that they are emperors without their clothes. Unbelievably, President Obama has appointed yet another of these Wall Street bankers as Secretary of the Treasury: Jack Lew, from Citi Group—a company whose stock went down to three dollars per share during the crisis. (Lew's predecessors were bankers Tim Geithner and Hank Paulson.)

I do not know Jack Lew personally, but I do know that executives from these big banks often get bonuses from their companies if they receive government appointments, and get their jobs back after their appointments expire. Their first loyalty is likely to their companies and their professions. They are not the only ones who can do this and other financial jobs in the government.

What these shysters truly deserve is to be in prison. In

addition, the bankers themselves should personally have to pay huge, meaningful fines for what they did. Why should their shareholders, alone, pay for their misconduct? A grand jury should be convened to determine if they should be indicted for criminal negligence, if not outright fraud. MFA, if we respectfully set aside crime victims who lost their lives or suffered bodily injury, my bet is that more people's lives have been damaged by these Wall Street bankers than by all of the crimes committed since they caused the financial crisis in 2008. If you doubt this, ask yourself: how many people do you know who have been victims of crime since 2008? Then compare that with the number of people you know who have lost their jobs, their homes, or their businesses, or have been otherwise seriously hurt by this man-made financial crisis.

Furthermore, these bankers gave themselves record salaries and bonuses as more and more people here and around the world suffered because of what they did. Criminals are forbidden from making money from books and movies about their crimes. Why should these bankers profit or even be rewarded for the destruction they caused? They should be stripped of their bonuses and salaries, and that money should be used to compensate their shareholders, and the other victims of their abuse.

However, to be fair, it is important to distinguish between the bankers at the very top of these Wall Street firms—the ones whose decisions caused this meltdown—and the rank and file employees. Like millions of other Americans, many of the latter lost their jobs as a result of the greed and mismanagement of their bosses—despite having to work hard and earn excellent grades in order to land one of these jobs. It is also necessary to draw a distinct line between the largest banks—the ones that had to be bailed out—and most of the small community banks and credit unions, which played no role in the financial crisis and remained safe and sound financially. In protest, more and

THE BANKS GOT HEROIC LIFE SUPPORT & DIDN'T DIE

SO STILL BORN FROM OR DEAD/ CLOSE

COMPANIES CAN BE

re. MONOPOLY FAILED

ARE NEW BONUS,

ARGUMENT AKIN TO FAIR 'START-UP' MARKET ARE START-UPS STRONG-

more Americans are switching their business and accounts to these smaller banks and credit unions. After what the big banks did to us, we all should.

The rest of the world looks to us for leadership on many issues, but especially for financial leadership. America is supposed to be the master of the game of free enterprise. The great wealth of our country rebuilt most of the world after the devastation of World War II. How do you think the world looks at us now that our alleged financial leaders on Wall Street duped it into making investments that were equally (or more) devastating to the international economy? These "leaders" have embarrassed our country and tarnished its reputation before the entire world. The financial turmoil playing out in Europe can also be traced back to the recklessness of these bankers. I'm not saying that Europe didn't have its own problems, but Wall Street worsened them into a full-blown crisis that threatens to take their economies and ours down again.

Even in the face of all of this economic destruction, the worst thing the big bankers have done is undermine the very integrity of our free enterprise system. It is no longer the same great merit-based engine of opportunity and prosperity for all Americans. They have corrupted it from the very top, making it no more than a stacked deck, where the rules and losses only apply to the rest of us suckers. Our economy should be running like the Ferrari that it is. These bankers abuse it as if it were a jalopy.

MFA, if these banks are too big to fail, then they are simply too big. To prevent this crisis from happening again, these oversized, bloated banks must be broken up so that the failure of one or a few of them can't drag down the economies of the entire world. Ten of the largest banks in our country control seventy-seven percent of all bank assets. As we have learned, that is dangerous. We cannot tolerate having a recession or depression

17% OF ALL BANK ASSETS

constantly hanging over our heads because a few greedy, irresponsible egomaniacs feel entitled to do anything they want.

The other thing that we must insist upon is that Congress
reinstates the Glass-Steagall law, which was originally passed
after the Great Depression. The purpose of this law was to prevent a similar financial disaster from ever happening again. What
the law did was to separate customer deposits from investment
banking. It forbade banks from using their customers' deposits
to make risky investments, so that the deposits would always
be safe and the banks would never again collapse. This law protected us for all these years until it was repealed in 1999 at
the behest of—you guessed it—the big Wall Street banks and
others, who used vast sums of money to finance an unrelenting
campaign to convince our (their) Congress, President, and other
policymakers that this law was antiquated and no longer needed.
Famous last words. Now, the only question is if we are going to
prevent this from happening to us again and again and again by
reinstating Glass-Steagall.

If the US is to maintain its status in the world, we have
to consistently be at the very top of our fiscal and economic
game. It is time for us to be brutally honest about our economic standing in the world. As has been the case throughout
history, there are countries that still want to dominate as much
of the world as they can. In the past, that domination was
attempted or achieved mostly through military force. Now, it is
about economic domination. This purely man-made, recession
has increased our already staggering national debt and made
us even more beholden to China as we borrow more and more
money from them.

China's foreign policies have shown that the only country
they care about is themselves. They have supported genocide in
Darfur. Only the threat of embarrassing them as the host of the
Olympics changed their minds. They have blocked every effort

No, CYBER DOMINATION

by the United Nations to stop the slaughter of innocent civilians in Syria. They can attempt to dress these policies up in as much diplomatic propaganda as they wish. However, in the end, they are nothing less than accomplices to murder. Do not doubt that they would be just as ruthless to us economically if they thought it was in their interest to do so. The more we borrow from them, the more leverage that they have over us. If we don't get our financial house in order, the day will come when China will use that leverage against us, and for the first time since the American Revolution, another country will dictate its policies to us and we will be number two.

BETRAYAL OF TRUST—THE GAME OF POLITICS HAS BECOME MORE IMPORTANT THAN OUR COUNTRY AND ITS PEOPLE

SHORTLY AFTER THE 2008 ELECTION, MITCH MCCONNELL, THE Minority Leader of the United States Senate, announced that his number one priority was to defeat President Obama in the next presidential election. At that time, our soldiers were being killed and wounded in two wars. The financial crisis was starting to cause the total collapse of our economy. We had the largest budget deficit in the country's history, and there was the ever-present possibility of terrorist attacks at home and abroad. In the face of these urgent, overwhelming problems, McConnell's number one concern was an election that was four years away.

Besides his incredibly misplaced sense of priorities, the Senator needs to be informed in no uncertain terms that our government is not about playing his juvenile, vindictive, insider political power games. Our government is not about him. Our government is not about the President. Our government is about the well-being of the country—and of us, the people.

We have seen this attitude acted out over and over, to our detriment. When terrorists attacked us on September 11, 2001, we all saw the unflinching courage and sacrifice of the first responders, who risked their lives (and lost them in some cases) to rescue the victims of this despicable act. Yet it took Congress nine years to pass a bill to help them and their families, and to compensate in some small way for their suffering and deaths. While waiting for our leaders to act on their behalf, hundreds of first responders have died of cancer and other chronic illnesses due to their exposure to the toxicity of that hallowed site. Many more are still getting sicker and dying because they did not get medical care sooner.

I can still remember some of our elected hypocrites in Washington giving emotional speeches on the floor of the House and Senate praising the first responders, only to turn their backs on them in their time of deepest need. Why did it take the Congress so long to act? The First Responders bill was held up because it was to be paid for by closing a tax loophole that allowed foreign multinational corporations to avoid paying taxes on income that they earned in our country. Does this represent your values?

THE ULTIMATE BETRAYAL

I T IS DIFFICULT TO WRITE ABOUT THIS BECAUSE IT EXPRESSES AN ATTI-tude toward us by some of our elected officials that is unthinkable even to the most cynical and jaded critics of our government and politics. Just when you thought it was impossible for them to treat us with more disdain and disrespect, they did. At the beginning of 2013, the Republican Tea Party controlled the House of Representatives and was actually willing to go on vacation without allocating the funds that were desperately needed by the victims of Hurricane Sandy (also known as "Superstorm Sandy"). As you know, the widespread damage and suffering from this storm was horrific. Aid and sympathy poured in from complete strangers all over the country. Yet the people that we pay to represent us in Congress were willing to walk away and leave millions of Americans hurting badly. This is beyond neglect. This is just plain mean. This is kicking people when they are down. This is giving the finger to Republicans, Democrats, Tea Party members, and everybody else. If there is any time when politics must be set aside, it is when our fellow Americans have been overwhelmed by a catastrophic natural disaster.

But not the jerks who are out of control with their ideology of insensitivity and outright hostility toward the people they are elected to serve.

My guess is that this was done, at least partly, to get back at the Governor of New Jersey, because he had the temerity to put politics aside and work with President Obama to help his state and its people recover from utter devastation. This sort of political revenge must stop, and we, the people, are the only ones that can stop it, by voting the offenders out of office. When a government starts being mean to its citizens, it is moving toward tyranny. That has no place in the United States of America. Sixty-seven House members voted against the Hurricane Relief Bill—all of them Republicans. After the vote they were shamed into reluctantly voting for a fraction of the money that was needed. Apparently, they could have cared less that some of the hurricane victims were Republican and Tea Party members.

However, their callousness didn't even stop there. They refused to extend the Payroll Tax Moratorium that was saving middle-class American families $1,000 per year in taxes. Their probable excuse was that we had to do something about the federal budget deficit. But don't believe that for a millisecond. First of all, most of these two-faced deceivers were the same ones who created this huge deficit in the first place. The fact is that when President Clinton left office, he left the country with a budget surplus. The current huge deficit was mostly created when the Republicans controlled the Presidency and both houses of Congress. They would have us believe that they are the party of thrift. What a joke. They insult our intelligence. Anyone who has paid any attention knows that while they were spouting the slogan "no new taxes," they were spending money as if there was no tomorrow. You don't need to be a Nobel Prize winner in economics to know that if you cut taxes and keep spending like crazy, you are going to create a huge deficit—which is exactly what they did. Then they tried to hide it. According to the Pulitzer Prize-winning *Guardian*, "By one estimate, 70% of the costs of wars in Iraq and Afghanistan between 2003 and 2008 were funded with supplemental or emergency appropriations approved outside the Pentagon's annual budget."[10] This is a process that bypasses traditional congressional budgetary oversight. The article goes on:

> More fundamentally, the Bush administration masked the cost of the war with deficit spending to ensure that the American people would not face up to its costs while President Bush was in office. Despite their recent discovery and outrage over the national debt, the Republicans followed the advice of Vice-President Dick Cheney that "deficits don't matter" and spent freely on domestic programs throughout the Bush years. The Bush administration encouraged the American people to keep spending and "enjoy life," while the government paid for the occupation of Iraq on a credit card they hoped never to have to repay.

The Republican-controlled Congress snatched $1,000 from every middle class family, yet they were willing to shut down the government and take the country's economy over the "fiscal cliff" rather than raise any taxes on the one percent that have more wealth than even multimillionaires can comprehend.

In 2001, President Bush signed into law a series of tax cuts. One measure cut the top income tax rate from 39.6 percent to 35 percent, and reduced capital gains and estate taxes. 93 percent of the recovery dollars went to the super-rich. The average tax cut of $520,000 went to the top 0.1 percent—those making more than $3 million a year.[11] The deficit exploded while the middle class fell further behind and those at the very top of the income scale walked away with the money. That is how pitiful we have become. Where is our self-respect? Where is our American Spirit? Where is the fight in us?

Don't be fooled. This is not about the federal deficit. This is about our elected officials pandering to some of the super-rich, who spend vast sums of money to help them win in the sad and destructive game of winner-take-all politics. If this was really about the deficit, there would be only one way to close it while doing the least damage to the country and its people. That would be to both cut spending and raise taxes. Those of us who have served at the state or local government level during hard economic times know this all too well. The reason is that state and local governments cannot engage in deficit spending. Unlike the federal government, each state constitution requires that the budget be balanced for every fiscal period. In other words, we cannot borrow money to pay for the ongoing operations of government. If there is not enough tax revenue, we must choose to raise taxes or make cuts. Usually, we have to do both to continue to provide the most vital services. There is forced discipline and the people expect us to be fair about whose taxes should be raised and what budgets should be cut.

Many of the members of our Congress have shown that they could care less about fairness. In fact, they are shameless advocates of unfairness. They all but refuse to vote money for sick and dying 9/11 first responders and for hurricane victims, while at the same time refusing to raise taxes on the very richest one percent of the population (those who have far and away benefited from the "economic recovery" the most), that pretty much says it all.

At this point, there are those who would accuse me of unfair partisanship against Republicans. However, if we are going to rid ourselves of the dysfunctional politics and politicians that are stifling the incredible potential of our country and its people, we must focus on the facts and not allow ourselves to be manipulated by propaganda, regardless of its source.

Many baby boomers may remember the television show *Dragnet*. The hero of the show was Police Sergeant Joe Friday. At the beginning of each episode, he interviewed an overly excited witness to a crime. After the witness had rambled on for a while, he would stop them and deliver his trademark line: "Just the facts ma'am, just the facts." That line applies even more to today's political landscape.

Millions and millions of dollars are spent to figure out how to push our buttons on any issue. These days, this is especially true with the advent of the Internet and social media. The speed and distance that information (or misinformation) can be spread is breathtaking. Any group, organization or individual can do it. This has greatly enhanced the use of one of the most insidious propaganda tactics of all time, "The Big Lie." This is the idea that if you tell people something enough times, they will begin to believe it, even if it is not true. A recent example was the persistent rumor that President Obama was not born in the United States.

With regard to the media establishment, even if you agree with *Fox News*, one must conclude that it is more about propaganda than news. For the first time in our history, a major television network devoted itself to outright propaganda. The Big Lie from *Fox News* was told at its inception with the slogan: "Fair and balanced, you be the judge." The network obviously had no intention of being either. Shortly afterwards, they had morphed into a TV version of their newspaper tabloids, with unrelenting attacks on anyone with views different from theirs. This was the brainchild of Rupert Murdoch, a super-rich guy who blew in from Australia and immediately set out to take over American politics. I wonder how Aussies would feel if some super-rich American tried to do that to their country. I suspect that he or she would figuratively if not literally end up as salt-water crocodile bait.

Some would say that something like *Fox News* is needed to counterbalance a supposed liberal bias of the media. Indeed, there should be balanced reporting by the media. At one time, it was the law in the United States that no one company was allowed to control all of the different types of media in a given market. This was because we recognized the power of the media to influence people's attitudes and opinions. If someone or some company can buy up all or most of the media in a given area, they can possibly control the politics of that area. Outside of the repeal of the Glass-Steagall law in the area of banking and finance, the repeal of these rules concerning media ownership was one of the most detrimental decisions ever made regarding fairness in American politics. Some would argue that it is even more egregious than the repeal of Glass-Steagall.

I contend that *Fox News* is different from others in the media because Rupert Murdoch wants to control our government, not just influence it. This is not paranoia. Again, look at the facts. Consider how Rupert Murdoch conducted his media empire in Great Britain. It's not just the unethical behavior of bribing police officers and hacking into people's voicemails for his tabloids. He seeks to get his people appointed to influential government positions. Elected officials in the UK fear that if they cross him, he will use the power of his empire to remove them from office. Sound familiar?

This is what makes Rupert Murdoch one of the most dangerous plutocrats of all. Not only does he have enough money to buy elected officials, he has a media empire that he viciously uses to bludgeon anyone he disapproves or disagrees with. Unlike most plutocrats, he is not content to use the government as a tool to make more money. He actually wants to run the government.

After a number of high-profile scandals, the British government actually held hearings to determine if Murdoch and his company, News Corp, were wielding undue influence over British politicians. Tony Blair, the former prime minister of Great Britain, testified that Murdoch wielded "substantial power" in Britain that had to be taken into account when devising political strategy and running the government. Needless to say, the UK is not some small, defenseless country. It is one of the most powerful nations in the world.

Blair further testified that Murdoch was critical to his own rise in politics. That is an understatement. Two years before the 1997 election for prime minister, Blair went to Australia to get Murdoch's blessing; he knew he could not win without it. Blair's relationship with Murdoch became so cozy that he actually became the godfather to one of Murdoch's children. There are serious allegations that Murdoch pressured Blair to join the United States in going to war against Iraq. However, when Blair would not do what Murdoch wanted on other matters, he testified that the *Daily Mail*, one of News Corp's tabloids, crossed the line. The former prime minister testified that they "attacked me, my family, my children, those associated with me, day out not merely when I was in office but subsequent to it as well." He further testified that "once they turn against you, that it is full on, full frontal, day in, day out, basically lifetime commitment." Sound familiar? Ask President Obama.

Blair was not the only former prime minister to testify about Murdoch's heavy-handed attempts to control the British government. Former Prime Minister John Major testified that Murdoch tried to influence his government's dealings with the European Union. He said Murdoch threatened that his newspapers would not support Major if he did not do what Murdoch wanted. Another former prime minister, Gordon Brown, testified that Murdoch's newspapers undermined British war efforts in Afghanistan.

These same hearings also focused on Blair's successor, David Cameron. Again, there is no doubt of Murdoch's attempts to exercise undue influence over Cameron's administration to get his way. At the time, Murdoch was trying to get permission from Cameron's administration to acquire even more media in Great Britain. That attempted acquisition was dropped by Murdoch when it became clear that it was not going to happen because of the scandalous conduct of News Corp, and especially its coziness with the Cameron administration. In 2010, Murdoch actually prevailed upon Cameron to appoint a former News Corp editor, Andy Coulson, as his media chief. Cameron did so even as the voicemail hacking scandal implicated the very newspaper that Coulson used to edit.

The voicemail hacking scandal engaged in by one of Murdoch's newspapers, *News of the World*, is one of the most egregious examples of unethical behavior that could be committed by the media. MFA, it resulted in the most expensive criminal trial in the history of Great Britain. It started when Murdoch's newspaper hired someone to hack into the voicemail of a young woman who had been murdered. As the trial proceeded, it turned out that thousands of British citizens' voicemails had been hacked. Dozens were arrested. Millions of dollars were paid out to settle civil lawsuits. Tony Blair's wife filed a lawsuit against News Corp for illegally tapping into her voicemail. Three executives from News Corp plead guilty. Andy Coulson was found guilty of conspiracy. It is believed that this was the first time a cabinet member of a British prime minister had been convicted of a crime. Prime Minister Cameron was forced to apologize to the people of Great Britain for his appointment of Coulson. Murdoch subsequently shut down *News of the World*.

This type of conduct epitomizes the unscrupulous, predatory mentality of News Corp and its founder.

Like the robber barons of Wall Street and the Koch Brothers, Murdoch seems to believe that if you have enough money and power, you can control a country's government without being elected or accountable to anyone. News Corp's attitude towards the American people can best be described by the comments of one of Murdoch's minions at *Fox News*, Bill O'Reilly. After President Obama won re-election, O'Reilly basically said that the people who voted for him were a bunch of deadbeats who only wanted government handouts. In other words, more than half of the American people were just lazy losers. How's that for arrogance and condescension?

Undaunted by the fiasco in Britain, Murdoch now wants to buy even more of the media to spread his propaganda. No person or corporation should hold that much influence over our country's politics. Fortunately for us, Murdoch withdrew his hostile bid to take over Time Warner—for now.

However, the most destructive thing about the *Fox News* propaganda machine is its relentless effort to divide the American people. Politics has been described as the art of compromise. This definition assumes that even though people on different sides of an issue may disagree, they will make a good faith effort to come to an agreement in order to benefit the people that they have sworn to serve. More importantly, it assumes that all sides genuinely believe that the people come first. I actually saw an interview of Speaker of the House John Boehner during which he was asked about compromising with President Obama. To the dismay of the interviewer, Boehner couldn't even get the word "compromise" to come out of his mouth.

With the mean-spirited attack dogs at *Fox News*, there is no such thing as compromise. They want their viewers to actually hate the people that they disagree with. They want anyone who disagrees with them to be seen as the enemy. Imagine what it would be like in your family, your workplace, or your circle of friends if everyone had this attitude. They would become completely dysfunctional and eventually disintegrate. In my view, this is exactly what *Fox News* wants to happen to this country, as long as they get what they want. Do you really believe that Rupert Murdoch is patriotic about our country? Of course not. If he was, he would be trying to bring us together rather than divide us as much as possible. In my opinion, he is here because this is the richest country in the world. He wants to control it in the same way that he controls in Great Britain, so that he can satisfy his obviously insatiable, maniacal appetite to have everything his way.

He is an American citizen, now, and he and his operatives are free to do as they please. Nevertheless, we must be wary of anyone who incessantly spews intolerance and tries to divide us. We Americans already have plenty that we disagree about. Many of our elected officials and some of the super-rich are trying to distract us while they rip us off. Don't believe them. Many of you may remember the "Two Minutes Hate" in George Orwell's novel *Nineteen Eighty-Four*.[12] In the book, Orwell writes about the daily ritual of "Two Minutes Hate," where the people of Oceania are made to watch a film depicting the "enemies" and scream hate at them. The purpose is to redirect people's anger and frustration away from the government that is exploiting them. FOX News does this with Obama, except it is twenty-four hours a day instead of two minutes.

One of the reasons our country is so great is that we are all free to speak our minds and express our ideas. Of course, there will be disagreements, but because you disagree with your spouse, family member, friend, co-worker, or fellow American doesn't mean that you have to hate them. The founders of our country came here to escape the intolerance of kings and queens. Freedom and intolerance cannot coexist.

The history of the United States of America has shown over and over again that when we are united as a people, there is no limit to the things our country can accomplish—whether it be saving the entire world from tyranny or landing on the moon. I'm not saying that we all need to hold hands with each other and sing "Kumbaya." However, if our country is to fulfill its truly unlimited potential with the great challenges it faces today, we must seek as much common ground as possible and demand that our elected officials end their needless bickering. They are hurting the people, making our government dysfunctional, and embarrassing us around the world. If they refuse to change, they must be thrown out of office. ARE YOU A GREAT AMERICAN?

LIBERTY
JUSTICE
PURSUIT
OF
~~HAPPI~~NESS

A NATION OF SHEEP

MFA, WHAT HAS HAPPENED TO US? HOW CAN WE BE SO PASSIVE IN the face of the injustice heaped upon the majority of us by the people we have elected? Where is the American spirit that made this country great? Are we willing to give up on one of the greatest ideals in the history of mankind—the American Dream? It sure looks like it.

Essentially, the American Dream boils down to three things: freedom, fairness, and a genuine opportunity to make a better life for ourselves. If any of these are missing, the Dream has failed. These principles are our right, as embodied by the United States Constitution. The purpose of government is to serve and protect these rights for all of us, not just a privileged few.

If our elected officials are unwilling to serve and protect the rights of all people, then they must be voted out. In a recent poll, our Congress had a seven percent approval rating. In your job, if you had a seven percent approval rating, you wouldn't have a job. Neither should these politicians. So how are they still in office? Because we don't care enough to hold them accountable, and they know it.

FABRIC WOULD UNRAVEL.

SO, W/OUR OUTSIDE PRESSURE · TO · DO THE SOCIALLY ACCEPTABLE THING — THE SOCIAL FABRIC

Love and gravity make the world go round, but it could not function without accountability. We are held accountable at work, in our families, and among our friends. We are even accountable to complete strangers because we have to do things like obey traffic laws. This condition applies to every facet of everyday life. If we don't do what is expected of us, there are consequences. We could be fired, ostracized, or imprisoned. We could even end up killing someone, or ourselves. Without accountability, there would be total chaos.

IE SOME WAY TO PIN THE BLAME ON SOMEONE

Because we are not holding our elected officials accountable, they have decided that they can do anything they want with impunity. They care more about their juvenile political games than about the country and the people. Republicans in congress refuse to even talk to the President, let alone negotiate with him about the serious challenges our country faces. It means nothing to them that the people re-elected him, because they don't care what "we, the people" think. To them, we don't count anymore.

Again, look at the facts. Even in the face of the tragic gun violence that plagues our nation, they do nothing. Ninety-one percent of Americans favor background checks for those who purchase guns. What does our Congress do? They vote it down. MFA, they're not just ignoring us, they are giving us the finger, and will continue to do so as long as we do not hold them accountable. They count on the fact that we are not watching what they are doing. To them, we have become irrelevant because no matter what they do or don't do, we keep re-electing them. From their point of view, all they have to do is throw a few sound bites and platitudes at us during election time with all of the money they raise, and they're in again. That is not their fault—it is ours. While we should be able to trust the people we elect to at least do no harm, we must face the reality that they have betrayed our trust.

Sadly, we must begin to think in terms of fear. We have to

make them fear us more than they fear the people who supply them with millions of dollars that have bought our government out from under us. In 2012, approximately $5.8 billion was spent to elect Congress and the President—$2.5 billion for the Presidency and $3.3 for the Congress. That is obscene. We should never allow ourselves to become desensitized by the ever-growing amount of money and the impact that it is having on the country.

MFA, the only thing that can trump all of this money is us, the people, with our votes. Our votes are the only thing more important to them than the money. Remember, the purpose of all this money is to get our votes!

Our votes are precious and powerful. We shouldn't treat them recklessly, or as inconveniences to be avoided or forgotten. The vote epitomizes what it means to be an American. This is how each of us has our say as to what our country is and will become. Our votes say we have the power over our government, not the other way around. It says that we are a free people with all the rights that every human being should have. It says that our country is fair because each of our votes count the same. It is our way of telling and reminding our elected officials that America is the land of opportunity and that the very purpose of our government is to give every American the opportunity to make a better life for themselves. And yet, voter turnout in the 2014 elections was the lowest since World War II. Only 36.3% of those eligible to vote used this most precious right. MFA, **we are abdicating our power to politicians and plutocrats who don't give a damn about us. We must take our right to vote back and exercise it.** Only thirty-five percent of African Americans turned out to vote in 2014. Though we followed the norm, we, more than anyone, should understand the importance of voting.

Earlier, I described the uprisings for freedom and justice in the Middle East and Northern Africa. Years later, people are still fighting and dying to have what we Americans take for granted.

In Egypt, the people were jubilant because they were sure they were on the path to having a full, true vote in their government. They elected a leader who they thought would bring them freedom and democracy. Instead, the will and dreams of the people were crushed, and they are right back where they started.

In South Africa, when apartheid fell after years of desperate struggle, many black South Africans waited in line for days in order to vote. People who have been deprived of the right to vote can remind us just how important it is, and how fortunate we are to have it.

We don't have to look overseas to understand that the vote is the ultimate expression of freedom and democracy. Under the repression of racial segregation in the south, the centerpiece of white southerners' efforts to keep us down was to deny us the right to vote at all costs. They used the law, intimidation, violence, and murder to keep us from voting. Once we were finally allowed to vote, white southerners did everything possible—including gerrymandering and other such methods—to make sure our votes didn't count as much as they should have. These methods are again being used today. White southerners understood that the vote was power. They knew that the vote was the great equalizer. They knew that if we could vote, it would be the beginning of the end of racial segregation. They were right. The passage of the Voting Rights Act in 1965 changed everything.

Today, almost fifty years later, the radical right is imitating the racists of a half-century ago, and they are doing it with the same demeaning attitude of superiority. By taking your right to vote away, they are saying you are inferior, and that you are not a real American. You really aren't good enough to vote. This time it's not just black people—it's anyone of whom they disapprove, or with whom they disagree. No one, certainly no American, should lie down and take that from anybody. That's why we had the American Revolution, to get would-be elitists off our backs.

In reality, elected officials such as these are simply unethical and dishonest. If they can't win an election on their merits, they cheat. This is like having the Super Bowl and locking members of the opposing team in the locker room. These are the kind of people who would be thrown in jail in Las Vegas for stacking the deck to cheat at cards. These are the kind of people who would deliberately try to break the legs of players on the opposing team in order to win. Worst of all, such elected officials are not even real Americans. They would be more at home in Russia, China, or North Korea, where they really know how to rig elections. In America, we should *encourage* people to vote.

It is not only important for the victims of this discrimination to stand up for their Americanhood—we should all stand up for the rights of our fellow Americans. In the African-American civil rights movement, there were the true leaders and heroes who put themselves in harm's way to show the cruelty and injustice of racial segregation to white Americans outside the south. However, it took the collective will of the majority of Americans, black and white, to move Congress to make racial discrimination illegal. It was a demonstration of the great power that We the People have, and how important it is for us to be aware of and exercise it, especially when our elected officials betray the trust we have bestowed upon them.

In some states, elected officials have passed laws solely to take away someone's rights to vote with no justification at all. They claim that they did it to prevent voter fraud. That is another of their "big lies." Again, the facts are that in every case their very own public officials in charge of running elections testified that they had experienced very little or no voter fraud at all. The only real fraud being committed is by the elected officials who say that this type of legislation is necessary. This is a diabolical solution to a problem that does not exist. It is only made worse by the US Supreme Court's political decision in 2013 to strike down the most important provisions of the Voting Rights Act that prevents discrimination at the polls. The Justices who voted for this decision must have wanted to make it even easier for their right-wing buddies to steal an election—as they did in the Bush vs. Gore presidential election, when black people were robbed of their votes, just like in the "good old days." Literally two hours after the decision was handed down, the Texas legislature passed their voter suppression legislation.

Their decision is an insult to all of the Americans throughout our country's history who stood up and put themselves at risk so that all of us could have the right to make the ultimate expression of what it means to be an American—especially to civilians and soldiers of all races who gave their lives for this cause. Also, we must never forget the long hard struggle of American women to get the vote. Men who were former slaves were allowed to vote before women could.

Growing up in Georgia prior to the passage of the 1965 Voting Rights Act, at election time I heard campaign ads that made it clear that the number one issue was who hated black people the most. You may know of the statement of George Wallace, the former Governor of Alabama, after he lost an election: "I will never be out-niggered again." After the passage of the Voting Rights Act, many of those very same politicians could be seen campaigning for votes in African-American churches and neighborhoods. Also, for the first time since Reconstruction, African-Americans began to be elected to public office. It was an amazing transformation to behold. Never underestimate the power of your vote.

In all fairness to Governor Wallace, before he died, he rolled his wheelchair into an African-American church in the middle of services and apologized for his racism in the front of the entire congregation. By all accounts, it was heartfelt and sincere.

KEEP 'EM POOR, UNDEREDUCATED, AND STRESSED OUT

THE DIABOLICAL ECONOMIC STRATEGY WHICH IS NOW BEING USED against the entire middle class, is easily recognizable to African-Americans who lived under segregation or any people who have lived under discrimination. Back in the days of slavery it was against the law to teach a black person to read. The reason was very simple. The idea was to keep them barely surviving, poorly educated, and too stressed out to figure out how to fight back. While the discrimination against the middle class is not as violent and obvious as it was under racial segregation, it is just as real and just as systematic. At least since the 1980s, the income of middle-class Americans has been declining when you factor in the cost of living. At the same time, the income of the top one percent has been growing exponentially. Incredibly, for the first three years of the post-2008 "recovery," ninety-five percent of income growth went to one percent of Americans.

Even after being decimated by the financial crisis, the middle class is still slowly but surely having the economic life strangled out of it. In August of 2013, only forty-four percent of Americans had full-time jobs, and that was down from 2012.

What is being done about it? Nothing. In fact, it is just the opposite. Republicans and their Tea Party cohorts in Congress—particularly in the House of Representatives—are blocking every attempt to encourage job growth for the middle class. Any number of initiatives have been put forth to stimulate the economy—economists of every persuasion agree they would be effective—yet Republicans in Congress refuse to even consider any of them. What are they willing to do? Shut down the government and default on debt that is backed by the full faith and credit of the United States of America. This is incomprehensible. Politically and financially, these people are bomb-throwing anarchists. They have made our government dysfunctional, and they are making our country dysfunctional as well. They don't care who or what they hurt in order to get their misguided way. Their only goals are to carry out their blood oath of attacking every initiative of President Obama, to kiss up to the super-rich who own them, and to punish the middle class and the poor.

I was the treasurer of just one of our states. However, the idea that any responsible public official would even speak of Oregon defaulting on its debt was inconceivable. That we would do so intentionally was even more so. The financial damage to our state and the damage to its reputation would be irreparable. Any state treasurer, regardless of party affiliation, would tell you the same thing. Yet, the members of the United States Congress are willing to embarrass our country in front of the entire world and risk economic shockwaves that could plunge the global economy into a depression. These people are dangerous. They must be removed from office.

They yap about the budget deficit. Any fool knows that one of the main ways to reduce the deficit is to put people back to work so they will pay taxes! They know that it is the small- and medium-sized businesses that are creating most of the jobs, not the largest businesses. If they can shovel $700 billion to the greedy incompetents on Wall Street, they can get financing to the businesses that create jobs. They should also be encouraging and funding people who want to start their own businesses. They know this, but they don't care. They would rather play their ridiculous political games. They also know that seventy percent of our economy is the middle class consumer. How can you suppress the income of seventy percent of the American people and expect to have a strong economy? By intentionally shrinking the middle class, they are killing the goose that lays the golden egg. Our battle cry must be, "We are the economy, stupid!"

The reason the economic recovery is so slow is because the people that the hacks on Wall Street put out of work haven't found new jobs. This shows just how stupid and perverted these plutocrats and obstructionists are. Obviously, the more money the middle class makes, the more money the super-rich make. The more decent-paying jobs and successful businesses people have, the more they spend. *REALLY ? THE HIGHEST PAY GOES TO THOSE WHO CONTROL THE*

The better educated and trained all Americans are, the more *HIGHEST* productive they are and the more value they add, which should *MONEY $!* mean better pay. For years, employers have been complaining *ITS NOT DUE TO* about the lack of skilled workers in this country—but this is *SMARTS.* because of insufficient funding of opportunities for training and higher education. We are not stupid. Those of us who have a job know that we are making some rich or super-rich person at the top even richer, while our wages have decreased or stagnated. We must demand a fair wage so we have a genuine opportunity to make a better life for ourselves also.

Henry Ford is obviously one of the greatest capitalists of all time. When he declared that he was going to pay his factory workers the unbelievably high wage, at the time, of $5 per day, many believed that it would destroy his company and even undermine free enterprise itself. As we know, the opposite happened. By paying his workers more, he solved his problem of excessive turnover caused by the monotonous working conditions on his assembly line and, most notably, his workers could then afford to buy his cars on installment. Unlike some of the less visionary and mean-spirited CEOs of today, Ford understood that investing in his employees instead of using them up and casting them aside like a waste product was good for his company, and the country. In economic terms, the American Dream is about every American, regardless of background, making more money if they are willing to improve themselves and work for it. Henry Ford was not only a titan of industry; he was also one of our nation's most generous philanthropists, who founded The Ford Foundation. However, because of his extreme words and conduct against the Jews, it must unfortunately be added that he was a rabid anti-Semite.

As to keeping the middle class less educated, as happened to black people under segregation—just look around your community. Tens of thousands of teachers have been laid off, and schools have been closed all over the country, due to the "greed fest" on Wall Street. MFA, this is about our children and their futures and therefore the future of the country. What is the response of our Congress? Nothing. Most don't even care about our children. Again, it is the Republican- and Tea Party-controlled House that is blocking everything. The administration and others in Congress have made proposals to repair the damage done to our schools by the recession, but their efforts have all been blocked and ignored by the House. To these people, absolutely nothing is above politics—unless, of course, it affects them personally. Did you notice what happened during the air-traffic controller problem caused by the "sequester" (a procedure by which across-the-board spending cuts go into effect if Congress fails to agree on a deficit-reducing budget by a specified date)? Flight delays were about to interfere with Congress's vacation, but they solved that problem in a few days.

There will be those who accuse me of blatant partisanship. This is not partisanship. It is a fact that the Republican- and Tea Party-controlled House is blocking every attempt to stop the middle class from shrinking into oblivion. It is they who refuse to understand that the education of our children and young people is too important to be some kind of political football. They are the party of "No."

If we can put our partisanship aside for just a moment, it is clear that these people are treating all of our children with disdain. Do you think that they have special uncrowded classrooms for middle class students whose parents belong to the Tea Party, or the Republican or Democratic Party? We must wake up and acknowledge that they don't care anything about the middle class, regardless of party affiliation or anything else.

How many times do we have to be spit in the face by these people before we understand this? They know that college students and their parents are carrying more than a trillion dollars in student loan debt—a crushing figure that has the potential to become another full-blown financial crisis for all of us. There is a bill that has been before Congress for months that would keep the interest rate from rising on loans to our neediest students. Yet the Republican-controlled House decided to go on vacation for the Fourth of July without taking up this bill, and let the interest rate rise. They seem to enjoy sticking it to us just as they go on vacation; consider for instance the payroll tax moratorium or the issue of aid for hurricane victims. No doubt, to add insult to injury. Just about every American, except these jokers, knows that education is the way to the American Dream for most of us. The money spent on education is an investment in us and our country—not just an expense. Actually, they know exactly what they're doing. They are deliberately trying to take the American Dream from us.

Another parallel to segregation and the current plight of the middle class is the persistent attempt to discourage students from going to college. Under segregation, we blacks could not go to school with whites, so most of the best colleges were off limits to us. Under the doctrine of "separate but equal," southern states had to provide colleges for us. While the role played by the traditionally black colleges and universities in overcoming racial discrimination cannot be overstated, they were allocated only a fraction of the resources of their white counterparts. The goal was always to make sure that our education was inferior.

If my single-parent mother had not earned her nursing degree from Tuskegee Institute (now Tuskegee University) we probably would have lived in poverty. She in turn sacrificed incredibly to give me the excellent education that allowed me to achieve things that would have been inconceivable to my grandmother. My grandmother could not read or write until my mother taught her to do so. My grandmother made ends meet by washing and ironing clothes for white people in the days before electric washing machines, dryers, and irons. Try telling us that education is not important. There is a good reason why Americans celebrate when a family member graduates, whether from grade school, high school, post-secondary training, college, or graduate school. They know that he or she has taken a big step toward a better life. It is a special celebration if the family member is the first to graduate, because the family knows what life is like without a good education. Knowledge is power. Knowledge opens the way to opportunity for a better life. Anyone who tells you otherwise is either sadly mistaken or lying.

My observation is that those who use the media to question the value of education are themselves well-educated and would not be in their positions without their education. Also, you can count on the fact that they are going to give their own children the best education possible. Some of these people are nothing more than mouthpieces for elitists in our society, who see the rest of us as nothing more than cheap labor whose main purpose in life is to serve their interest and make them richer. This is not paranoid conspiracy theory. It is the history of African-Americans in our country. While slavery was the embodiment of racial prejudice, injustice, and cruelty, it was also about economics. Since we weren't paid, we were the cheapest labor that could be had. Even after the Civil War, when we were technically freed, very little actually changed for most African-Americans in the south. One system of slavery was replaced with another. Under the law, if an African-American was unemployed (i.e. not working for their former master) they could be arrested for vagrancy. While in jail, they were hired out as free labor for white people. This went on for years, well into the twentieth century. Nevertheless, we never lost sight of the fact that education was our main way of getting out of poverty.

LESS EDUCATION EQUALS CHEAP LABOR

H AVE NO DOUBT THAT THERE IS A DELIBERATE ATTEMPT BY SOME OF our elected officials at all levels of government to deprive most Americans of educational opportunities so that their super-rich supporters can pay us less for our work. Once again, look at the facts. They tell the "big lie" that a college education isn't worth the investment. They point to the fact that so many college graduates are unemployed. How stupid do they think we are? The reason college graduates don't have jobs is the same reason that millions and millions of Americans lost their jobs. The prosperity destroyers on Wall Street all but killed the economy. If it were not for their greed, the jobs would have been there, and young peoples' educations would have had them well on their way to getting their piece of the American Dream.

To college graduates and those who want to go to college: don't let anybody denigrate what you have achieved or cause you to question your ambition to make a better life for yourself. There is nothing wrong with getting a college degree or more education and training. Indeed, in today's world it is essential. The problem is that there are some people in our country who feel that the American Dream is just for a chosen few—and there are elected officials, especially in Washington, who are doing their bidding. Get involved and vote them out of office, and put in some people who understand that our quality of life and the greatness of our country are dependent on an excellent educational system for all Americans.

Some politicians are so self-obsessed that they fail to grasp that there is a hungry, ambitious world that is gaining on us. If we are to maintain our preeminence in the world, we need the talent, skill, and brainpower of all of our people, regardless of background. Again, as the saying goes, there is no power without brainpower. Discriminating against people and withholding educational opportunities is no longer an option. As I look back on my own childhood, I am sad to think of the talent that was wasted due to lack of educational opportunities caused by racial discrimination. The parents of so many of my friends could not make the kind of sacrifices that my mother made for me. Then I think of the lost talent of half of our population, due to discrimination against women and other groups. America truly is the land of opportunity. There is plenty for all of us. Education is the great equalizer that helps us to seize it. Don't let these elitists dummy us down. Are you a Great American? Then vote them out!

"RIGHT TO WORK" MEANS THE RIGHT TO GET CHEATED OUT OF A FAIR WAGE

WE NEED A 'WRONGFUL WORK' MEME THAT CAPTURES THE DISVALUE OF A LABOR LAW.

ONCE AGAIN, THOSE WHO WANT TO PAY WORKERS LESS THAN THEY deserve are using propaganda and deceptive language to hide their true intent. This time, the words are "right to work". They imply that someone or something is trying to take your work away from you. This is sheer nonsense. Slaves had the "right to work". Their problem was that they didn't have the right to get paid. Today, the right to work is simply a ploy to destroy or weaken unions. In situations where most of the workers are represented by unions, all workers have to pay union dues even if they don't actually belong to the unions. The rationale for this is that all workers get the increased wages negotiated by the union, so all should pay their fair share of union dues.

The dispute between management and workers is long-standing. It is not an exaggeration to say that in times past it has been more like a war. Very few Americans are alive today who remember violent clashes that occurred when management hired private militia to crush any attempt by workers to unionize. Many were seriously injured or killed. The intensity of the violence is best described by what happened at what is called the Battle of Blair Mountain, which occurred in the 1920s, in West Virginia. Coal industry management actually hired airplanes that dropped bombs on coal miners who were attempting to unionize. In the dispute, thousands of armed coal miners faced off against thousands of strike breakers and lawmen. More than a million rounds of ammunition were fired. The United States Army finally had to intervene to stop the bloodshed. This is how hard workers have had to fight management for decent treatment.

The coal companies all but owned the miners. They controlled every aspect of the miners' lives. Not only was the pay extremely low, but the working conditions were deadly. Between 1890 and 1912, coal miners in West Virginia had the highest death rate in America. 1000 miners died. Many more were seriously injured. The coal companies refused to adopt safety standards because it would cut into their profits. Children as young as nine years old worked in the mines.

Many of the things that we take for granted today are the result of union representation. Before unions there were no weekends without work. Before unions there was no eight-hour workday or forty-hour work week. Before unions there were no breaks at work—including lunch breaks. Before unions there were no child labor laws. Before unions there were no paid vacations, paid holidays, or overtime pay. However, today the main issue is pay. The fact is that in the twenty-five states with "right to work" laws, workers earn $5,971 dollars less a year than workers in other states. Median household income in these states is twelve percent less than the other states.

The reason that plutocrats like the Koch brothers and others attack unions is very simple. The less money that workers make the more money they make. They refuse to acknowledge that it is the workers who are making them rich and are therefore entitled to make more money as well. That is why unions came into existence in the first place. The stagnation of the income of the middle class is evidence that the unions are still needed. Again, when was the last time you got a raise?

GOVERNMENT OF THE MONEY, BY THE MONEY, FOR THE MONEY

T_{HE ABOVE IS A MODIFICATION OF SOME OF THE GREATEST WORDS} ever spoken in our nation's history: the Gettysburg Address, by Abraham Lincoln. His actual words were as follows: "and that government of the people, by the people, for the people shall not perish from the earth." Unfortunately, the former language is a more accurate description of what our government has become today.

As a former elected official, I know that politicians are the easiest targets for criticism, and much of the time, deservedly so. Nevertheless, we must be fair and try to understand the incredible pressure that candidates are under to raise campaign money. I will use myself as an example. I served ten years in the Oregon legislature—two terms (four years) in the House and six years in the Senate—before being elected State Treasurer. The centerpiece of my legislative campaigns was a relentless door-to-door effort by me, personally. My goal was to knock on every door in my district, myself. I only needed an adequate amount of money for the other forms of political advertising to supplement my goal of meeting as many people as possible on their doorsteps.

Things changed tremendously when I ran for State Treasurer. You can't knock on every door in the state. It became a media campaign. Television is expensive. Suddenly, I had to raise at least ten times more than I did as a legislative candidate. When I ran unsuccessfully for Governor, the pressure was even greater. I had to spend at least six hours a day "dialing for dollars." It was excruciating. When I woke up in the morning, my stomach would tighten into a knot just thinking about it. I had to raise at least one million dollars to have any chance of winning. Day after day was spent begging for money. I hated it.

For years, campaign spending has been increasing exponentially to the point of absurdity. It will continue to do so unless we stop it. Campaign finance reform will not come from the politicians. They are prisoners of the present system because they know how it works and they have made it work for themselves. For them, changing it would be too risky. Change must come from the outside—from us. We must tell our politicians to pass meaningful campaign finance reform or we'll throw them out of office, and we must really mean it.

Members of Congress in the House of Representatives must run every two years. They must raise hundreds of thousands, if not millions of dollars every time. Consequently, most of them spend more time raising campaign money than doing anything else—including the business of the country.

As soon as one campaign is over, they have to start raising money for the next one. Needless to say, there is tremendous pressure to get large contributions from as few sources as possible. You especially want to keep your big donors happy because you are going to need their help again very soon. Even though Senators only have to run every six years, their campaigns must cover the entire state. Senators from the most populous states can easily spend tens of millions of dollars on their campaigns. The point is that as campaigns become more and more expensive, members of Congress have become so preoccupied with raising money that it overshadows their responsibility to the country and the people. To them We the People are irrelevant, because they fund their campaigns with donations from the rich and powerful special interests and individuals, and they know that we won't hold them accountable no matter how poor their performance is or even how much they insult and hurt us. They count on our ignorance and apathy. They know that they have a seven percent approval rating. "So what?" they think. They know we are going to keep reelecting them anyway, because we just keep doing it time after time. We are like dogs that they keep kicking because we never bite back. They use their campaign money to manipulate us by playing to our fears and prejudices, and we just eat it up—to our own detriment. We must force them to pass campaign reform legislation to keep our government from sinking into total corruption. Are you a GREAT AMERICAN? Will you bite back?

In the 2012 election, casino billionaire Sheldon Adelson gave away $100 million to candidates. In a Las Vegas meeting dubbed the "Adelson primary" because of the billionaire's outsized influence on Republican campaigns, presidential hopefuls like New Jersey governor Chris Christie, Wisconsin governor Scott Walker, Ohio governor John Kasich, and former Florida governor Jeb Bush fell all over themselves to be among the "show ponies" at Adelson's circus. To his credit, Adelson commented to *Forbes* in 2012 that he was against very wealthy people influencing elections. "But as long as it's doable," he added, "I'm going to do it."[13] MFAs, without campaign finance reform we will have government of the plutocrats, by the plutocrats, and for the plutocrats. The rest of us can perish from the earth, for all they care.

YOU MAY ELECT THEM, BUT WE OWN THEM

ONE OF THE WORST THINGS THAT HAS HAPPENED TO OUR GOVERN-ment as a result of the "winner take all" politics that has engulfed us is the politicization of our judiciary. If we cannot get fairness and justice from our courts, then we are no better than the totalitarian governments around the world where the rule of the law means nothing. Constitutional law was my favorite subject in law school because it showed how our country was shaped by one of the most wonderful and important documents in the history of mankind (and womankind): the United States Constitution. We read opinions by justices of the Supreme Court who were considered liberal, conservative, and in between. Regardless of their political and philosophical leanings, they respected legal precedent because it showed the thinking of pre-vious justices who wrestled with the same difficult issues. Now, we have some people on the court who are nothing more than politicians in robes. They are more interested in toeing the party line than respecting the evolution and progression of our laws.

The case in point is the Citizens United opinion. Among other things, this opinion allowed the formation of Super

PACs—political action committees that could anonymously contribute unlimited money to candidates. Let me be clear: this decision held that individuals and organizations, including corporations, could contribute money to our senators and representatives without reporting who or where the money came from. The idea that our highest court would say that We the People have no right to know where our elected officials get their money from is outrageous! MFA, there are really only two ways that you can know what a politician really stands for—their voting record and who they get their campaign money from. I submit to you that sometimes you can learn more about a candidate by knowing who they get their money from than by studying their voting record. This is obviously true for first-time candidates who have no voting records. When I was a candidate in Oregon, I had to report every contribution over $25. I had to identify the contributor, their occupation or type of organization, and the amount. If we ever needed transparency, we need it for political money, especially in Congress, today.

Literally anyone can form a Super PAC. You and I could form one. The problem is that so could a foreign country or organization that is hostile to our national interest. MFA, Al-Qaeda or ISIS could form a Super PAC without us knowing it. The question is why would the Supreme Court allow this? They could have decided this case without even coming close to such a startling determination. To say that they overreached is a gross understatement. My opinion is that they made this decision so that wealthy individuals and corporations could contribute huge sums of money to conservative causes and candidates without the general public's knowledge. They were afraid that if people found out these individuals and corporations were working against them, they would stop buying or encourage a boycott of their products.

Not too long ago, the CEO of Chick-fil-A spoke out publicly

against gay marriage. While I absolutely disagree with his position, at least he had the courage to state his position publicly, even if it might hurt his company. Many individuals, organizations, and public companies take stands on controversial issues. To me, the people who hide behind these Super PACs are cowards, who once again think that their money entitles them to some kind of special privilege to have undue influence over our government without the rest of us knowing about it. This is a free country and they have the right to use their money to express their political views—but not in secret. In a democracy the American people are entitled to know who is giving money to the officials we elect. All contributions should be reported. Congress can vote to make this happen. If they don't, we need a new Congress. Are you a Great American who is prepared to vote them out if they don't tell us who they get their money from?

SOUNDS RIGHT — IN ORDER TO KEEP ELECTIONS HONEST, BUT WHERE IN THE CONSTITUTION IS THIS ADDRESSED?

SO, WHEN DEMS RETAKE CONGRESS, WE CAN CLEAN THIS UP — PROVIDING IT ISN'T UNCONSTITUTIONAL TO PUT LIMITS ON PRIVATE CONTRACTS BETWEEN PUBLIC OFFICIALS & PRIVATE ENTITIES. THIS SHOULD NOT BE PROBLEM — OFFICIALS CAN'T WORK IN CONFLICT OF INTEREST.

PIMPING FOR PLUTOCRATS

IF YOU DON'T KNOW WHO KARL ROVE AND GROVER NORQUIST AND their ilk are, you should. These unelected individuals have almost complete control over many of the Republicans in Congress and therefore our Federal government as a whole. In and of themselves, they have no power. Basically, they are nothing more than front men. What gives them their inordinate influence is, of course, the hundreds of millions of dollars given to their Super PACs by super-rich individuals and corporations who want to control our government for their advantage, and at our expense. Many of our elected officials are more than willing to sell us out. What is worse is that we just bend over and let them get away with it. Unfortunately, many of our elected officials have sold their souls, and sold us out.

You may have heard how Grover Norquist got many of the Republicans in Congress to sign a written oath that they would not vote to raise taxes. Whether or not you agree with the idea of no new taxes, you must admit that it is absolutely unacceptable for an individual citizen to have enough control over a member of Congress—someone elected by the people—to require them

THIS IS A CONFLICT OF INTEREST

to take an oath. There is only one oath that should matter to a politician, and that is the oath of office he or she takes when sworn in. That oath is to the Constitution of the United States. No individual should have the power to lock a member of Congress into any position, or to limit their ability to vote as they see fit. While it is the senator or representative who casts the vote, that vote belongs to the people he or she represents, and it is they (and only they) that the member should be accountable to.

So what happens to the senator or representative who refuses to vote or do as they are told? The Super PAC enforcer takes them aside and threatens to withdraw their financial support—or, even worse, to find a candidate to run against them in the next Republican primary. It's the political equivalent of "do what I say or I'll bust your knee caps."

The only difference is that these thugs use money as their weapon, instead of a sledgehammer or a crowbar. When your senator or representative yields to these threats—as most of them apparently do—he or she no longer represents you or the country. He or she represents the people with the money. This is the essence of how money is undermining and corrupting our democracy. This is how our government is being bought out from under We the People. While many Republicans in Congress are experiencing blatant coercion and intimidation by big money, there is no doubt that Congress as a whole, regardless of party affiliation, is absolutely and unduly influenced by the incredible amounts of money that flow into our nation's capital. I dare say that hardly a vote is cast or position taken that is not first and foremost evaluated in terms of receiving or not receiving campaign money.

The reason that they ignore us and cater to the super-rich is because we don't give them the huge amounts of money they are obsessed with, and we just keep voting for them again anyway. If our country is going to be a democracy instead of a plutocracy, we must demand campaign finance reform, and each of us must use our vote to hold them accountable. Are you a Great American?

As a Democrat, I probably have no business commenting on the internal workings of Republican politics. However, if you are a Republican, it must be said that the super-rich and big corporations have taken your party from you, both to its detriment and the detriment of our country. One of the reasons Mitt Romney lost was because he had to spend most of the Republican primary fighting off opponents who would have been out of the race but for the money of a few very wealthy contributors. The attacks on him were relentless, and more negative than anything he faced from President Obama. Also, most of the super-rich supported a far-right agenda that Romney had to appease, leaving the moderates to President Obama.

However, the main reason why I say that the takeover of your party is detrimental to the country is because I simply do not believe that most rank-and-file Republicans approve of the dysfunction in our government that is being caused by the mean-spirited intransigence of the far-right wing. Regardless of party affiliation, most Americans want our government to move the country forward, away from the bitter, needless stagnation that we are in now. When I was first elected to the Oregon Legislature in 1982, I represented the second-most Republican district in the state. The Senate district that I represented was also predominantly Republican. African-Americans made up approximately three percent of Oregon's population at that time. Ninety-five percent of that three percent lived in the state's largest city, Portland. I live in Salem, the state's capital— and an overwhelmingly white city. Yet over thirty years ago, the people of my districts elected (and re-elected) me, a black Democrat. During my service in the legislature, we had our battles, but I can honestly say that Republicans and Democrats always put the people first by working to put our political differences aside as much as possible and looking for common ground on the issues facing our state. Oregonians—whether Republicans or Democrats—expected no less of us. I believe that most Americans of both parties feel that way today. It is time for us to put an end to this nonsense, and throw out any politicians who refuse to put the country and the people first. Are you a Great American? Then pull the lever.

BARACK AND JACKIE

P ERHAPS THERE IS NO ASPECT OF OUR SOCIETY THAT MORE CLEARLY reflects our country's history than our sports. This is definitely true when it comes to racial history of America. Most people are familiar with the story of Jackie Robinson, the first African-American to play major league baseball. He was greeted with the strongest racial prejudice and outright hatred. He became a symbol to black Americans of what happens to the first of us to break the color line in a given domain: get ready to catch hell.

On the other hand, most people are not familiar with Jack Johnson. He was the first black heavyweight boxing champion of the world. At first, white fighters refused to fight him because of their racism. They referred to him with the "n" word. However, when enough prize money was offered to Tommy Burns, the reigning champion, the fight was held. When Jack Johnson won, race riots broke out all over the country. Hundreds of African Americans were attacked and murdered from coast to coast. The public cried out for a "Great White Hope" to take the title back. And when Hank Aaron, the African American baseball player, was getting close to breaking Babe Ruth's home run record, he received threats that he would be killed if he broke it. These are just a very few instances of how racial bigotry has played out in our sports history. Here we are only talking about sports. How do you think present-day bigots feel about a black man becoming President of the United States?

I did not think that I would live to see an African American elected President in my lifetime (unless, of course, it was me). President Obama's election was historic and amazing. It removed any doubt as to whether the American people as a whole fully embraced the principles upon which our country was founded. To many Americans it signaled the end of racial prejudice in our country. However, many of us who grew up "back in the day" knew better. Prejudice does not go away at the flip of a switch. This young man's troubles were just beginning. We knew that the Jackie Robinson syndrome was still alive and well.

CONGRESSIONAL RACISM—"I REFUSE TO ACKNOWLEDGE THAT A BLACK MAN IS PRESIDENT"

LET'S JUST COME OUT AND SAY WHAT EVERYBODY KNOWS ANYWAY. There are people in our country who simply cannot stand the fact that an African American is the President of the United States. This is straightforward racism. As you would expect, there are members of Congress who feel the same way. The difference is that everyone knows that President Obama came into office facing difficulties our country had not experienced since the Great Depression. We were in two wars, and the economy was on the verge of collapse. President Obama has guided the economy back from the brink, and we are disentangling ourselves from two wars (which shouldn't have happened in the first place). On the basis of these two accomplishments alone, he would be regarded as a hero if he were white. Whether or not the American people as a whole regard him as a hero, they thought he did a good enough job to honor him with reelection in the face of the most well-financed and fierce opposition in the history of presidential politics, and some of the most negative campaigning ever.

Some will say that I am just another black man "playing

the race card." Once again, look at the facts. In the Senate, the Republicans have filibustered against sixteen of Obama's nominees for various government posts. In the entire previous history of the country, there have only been eight filibusters against a president's nominees. This is extreme, even for politicians from the Republican Tea Party, who have already demonstrated that they are angry and tend to hate everybody—except, of course, for the super-rich benefactors who finance them.

Earlier, I mentioned that the Senate Minority Leader Mitch McConnell stated his number one priority was to defeat President Obama's reelection even though the country was facing some of its greatest challenges ever. Under those circumstances, his remarks were extreme. How do you think he felt after losing again in 2012? After all, he resorted to some of the most vindictive uses of the Senate rules in its history. Is the Senator's conduct racially motivated? I don't know what's in his mind, but he sure acts like it. Actually, I could care less about his motivation. He is just one more in a long line of politicians who want to keep black people in their place. What I do know is that his vendetta, and that of some of his colleagues, has made our government a ridiculous, dysfunctional spectacle that is unnecessarily hurting and dividing our country. I also know that he was a leader in the government that got us into the mess that President Obama inherited. That makes him (and his cohorts) absolute hypocrites.

However, the most disturbing thing about these ultra-right-wing Republicans is their arrogant disregard of the will of the people. Whether they like it or not, the people have spoken. They reelected the President. Until now, a direct vote by the people has always been given the highest respect by elected officials because it is the purest form of our democracy. Imagine that you have elected the governor of your state and the members of your state's legislature tell you that they absolutely refuse to negotiate or work with him or her about any issues facing your state. While this would be an insult to your governor, the most serious consequence would be the lack of respect for the vote or the will of the people. If our vote means nothing, then we no longer have a democracy.

We now know from former US Senator George Voinovich (R) of Ohio, who served with McConnell and was in office when Obama was first elected, that McConnell started plotting against Obama even before he took office. Voinovich was quoted as saying the Republicans in the Senate and House of Representatives received orders (no doubt from the Koch brothers) that "if he (Obama) was for it, we had to be against it."[14] MFAs, this is the political equivalent of declaring war—not only on the President, but even worse, on the country as well. The record shows this is exactly what they have done. To them, it doesn't matter whether what Obama proposes is good for the county. This is a sick, hateful abdication of duty to the American people.

Voinovich was considered to be a true political conservative. He turned whistleblower when his fellow republicans blocked a bill that would have helped small businesses get loans and create jobs to get us out of the recession. He said that we don't have time for their games any longer. This bill is just one example of the many initiatives that were put forth by the Obama administration (and others) that would have stimulated the economy and helped put people back to work. But these initiatives were killed by the Republicans for the sole purpose of making Obama's presidency a failure, no matter what.

My personal experience with such attitudes hardly rises to the level of showing complete disrespect to the President of the United States, but I do have personal experience dealing with a politician like McConnell. It came when I was attending a Catholic elementary school in Atlanta: Our Lady of Lourdes. The Catholic schools were racially segregated, just like the public schools. One year, the Catholic schools put on a program at the old Atlanta Municipal Auditorium, which was attended by all of the students and teachers. In part it featured students making presentations to the Mayor of Atlanta, William B. Hartsfield. I was chosen to make the presentation for our school. When the time came, a little white girl and I stood side by side on the stage in front of the mayor. She made her presentation, and afterwards the mayor shook her hand. Then I made my presentation. Afterward, I stuck out my hand, and in front of all of those people, the mayor refused to shake it. It takes a big man to snub an eight-year-old. Just like it takes a real statesman to put his racial prejudice ahead of what is best for the country.

Our far-right-wing Republican-controlled House of Representatives has become like a nursery school of petulant, spoiled brats, whose idea of doing the country's business is throwing tantrums. They have voted over forty times to repeal ObamaCare. To do the same thing over and over again expecting a different result is a definition of insanity. How about some votes for creating good-paying jobs? How about some votes for rehiring laid-off teachers and lowering tuition costs? How about some votes for our military and their families that are being hurt by underfunding and mismanagement? What about any vote on anything to show that you care about something other than being mean to the people who elected you, humiliating the president that we re-elected and embarrassing our country in front of the entire world?

When the Tea Party first came onto the scene, I kept an open mind, because I thought that they were truly a grass roots organization. At first, I wasn't sure what they stood for, but I admired the fact that that at least they were standing up for something. When they first came out against ObamaCare, I still reserved judgment until I could fully understand what they were about.

When the financial crisis occurred in 2008, I got my answer. When millions of people started losing their jobs, businesses, homes, savings, and retirements, I expected Tea Partiers to show up on Wall Street with torches and pitchforks to give those bankers the kinds of bonuses they really deserved. After all, by this time the protests against ObamaCare had become vicious. I waited and watched. There was not a peep out of the Tea Partiers. That is when I knew the group was not anything like what it appeared to be. Let me say this as plainly as possible: if you claim to be a grass roots organization that stands up for the average American and you are not outraged enough to protest the damage done to so many Americans—including Tea Party members—by those big banks on Wall Street, then you are not standing up for anybody, not even yourself. Of course, we now know that the group is a creation of the Koch Brothers, and was designed to relentlessly attack President Obama.

So why do busloads of people show up to protest ObamaCare and not the almost complete destruction of the economy? Because ObamaCare is just a straw man for refusing to accept a black man as President. It is straightforward racial prejudice. If it were not ObamaCare, it would have been some other issue. Every time a racial injustice occurs in this country, people say that America needs to have a "conversation" about race—as if people don't know what racism is. Well, here it is. There is still a lot of racism and prejudice in our country. That's it. What else is there to say? These people hate Obama because he is black and because he defeated them and their prejudice by getting elected and re-elected President of the United States. They espouse the same blind hatred that Jackie Robinson once had to put up with. They want to attack, humiliate, and punish the president as much as possible, and at all costs. What a surprise.

What is truly surprising is that at this point in our history, their hatred is so extreme that they are willing to hurt the country in order to get back at him. This is where the line must be drawn. The well-being of the United States of America must come before our prejudices. These mean, selfish, pigheaded people are weakening our country economically, and trashing its reputation around the world—and they don't care. Their bigotry means more to them than our country does.

Look at what they are doing to Americans in their everyday lives. You don't have to be a psychiatrist or psychologist to see the stress that most Americans are under just to make ends meet. Any fool knows that the number one priority should be improving the economy. They should be creating decent-paying jobs by helping small and medium-sized businesses grow. They should be encouraging people to start their own businesses.

They should also be investing in education and training, so that people can make more money by adding more value to their work. For years, employers have been complaining about the lack of skilled workers. They should be hiring back thousands of teachers that have been laid off. They should be giving parents and students relief from crushing student loan debt. Yet these contemptuous people would rather have us suffer and our country weakened than work with the "n" word in the White House. MFA, third world countries are making fun of us as these lunatics try to divide us and drag us down. We are so much better than this.

We don't need to have a conversation about race. What We the People need to decide is whether acting out our racism and prejudices is more important than moving this great country forward and putting people in office who want to unite us and bring out the best of America, instead of dividing us by appealing to our fears and prejudices.

I know that some people believe what they want to believe—even if it is totally irrational and the facts say otherwise. For example, when some Republicans in Louisiana were polled about who was responsible for the Hurricane Katrina rescue and recovery debacle, more of them blamed President Obama than blamed President Bush, who was in office at the time. You really have to hate someone to blame him for something you know for a fact he was not responsible for. When people act on these kinds of beliefs, it tears at the soul of what our country stands for, because it is blatantly unfair. Nevertheless, I have no doubt that they love this country. What makes someone a "Great American" is putting what is best for our country first.

Unlike Woodrow Wilson, an unmitigated bigot who wouldn't even let black soldiers fight for our country—he lent them to the French army, where many received France's highest military honor, the Croix De Guerre—President Truman ordered racial integration of our armed forces, though many in the military were absolutely opposed to it. Yet this action succeeded because it was the best thing to do in order to have the strongest military in the world. Teamwork and maximum utilization of every soldier's skills are more important than racial prejudice when you have to win a war to protect the country and save lives.

The same was true for the integration of sports. When I was growing up in Georgia, not only did white colleges and universities refuse to have black players on their teams—they refused to play against a team that had a black player on it. That has all changed, primarily because if you don't put the best players on the field or court and have them play as a team, you will not win. As simplistic as it sounds, the same basic principle applies to our country. Are we willing to put our differences aside as much as possible so that our country can achieve its unlimited potential? That is what it takes to be a "Great American." By the way, the Louisiana State University Tigers have done pretty well since the teams integrated.

As for those who feel it necessary to hate the President of the United States because he is black: go ahead. Hate me too.

WE SHOULD HAVE STAYED W/ UNIVERSAL COVERAGE! IF WE HAD MORE FULL TIME EMPLOYMENT, MAYBE IT WOULDN'T BE SUCH A PROBLEM, BUT IF 6 OUT OF 10 WORKERS NOT QUALIFYING FOR HEALTH BENEFITS DUE TO PART TIME STATUS. WE NEEDED TO DO SOMETHING DRASTIC.

* THE GOP CRIPPLED THE TROUBLE IS, IT WOULD SURELY UNDERPERFORM

* HILARY DID A GREAT DEAL OF THE HOME WORK TO GET IT ROLLING! SO TRUST IT

I'm black. Every day millions of Americans go out into the world knowing that many of their fellow Americans disapprove or even hate them for reasons that have nothing to do with their character or ability. Personally, I couldn't care less. We get on with our lives. In America everyone is free to think and feel as they please. However, I believe that I can speak for most of us "minorities" in saying that we will never, ever again accept anybody acting out to deprive us of our full rights as Americans. Those days are over.

Instead of wasting your time and energy hating us, you had better focus on what is happening to you, your family, your friends, and your community. If you are middle class, you are being decimated, and not by Obama or any of us "minorities." It was done by a bunch of greedy white men on Wall Street, and is being done to you by another bunch of greedy, super-rich, power hungry white men who care as little about you as they do about us.

None of us are going anywhere. We are all in this together whether we like it or not. If we put the well-being of our country first, we all win. ARE YOU A GREAT AMERICAN? And most importantly, vote people into office that will put the country and the people first. If they can't do that, they don't deserve the honor of being there.

I am not saying that all Tea-Party Republican members are racist, or that the only reason that some oppose ObamaCare is because it was his idea. It's possible that some Tea Party Republicans have genuine political grievances that have nothing to do with race or President Obama in particular. Having said that, I must ask: where was their outrage when President George W. Bush was running the economy into the ground and getting us involved in two unnecessary wars? I say without reservation that the Tea Party Republicans in Congress are conducting them-selves in a way that indicates that their true agenda is protecting the super-rich, blocking every attempt by President Obama to accomplish anything, and attacking middle-class Americans. My litmus test, again: what are they doing to help reign in Wall Street's oversized banks and prevent another financial crisis? The answer: nothing. That shows me exactly who they are really working for. Again, if you are (or used to be) a middle-class American, I don't care what your party affiliation, skin color, gender, or anything else is—Tea-Party Republicans in Congress are working against you.

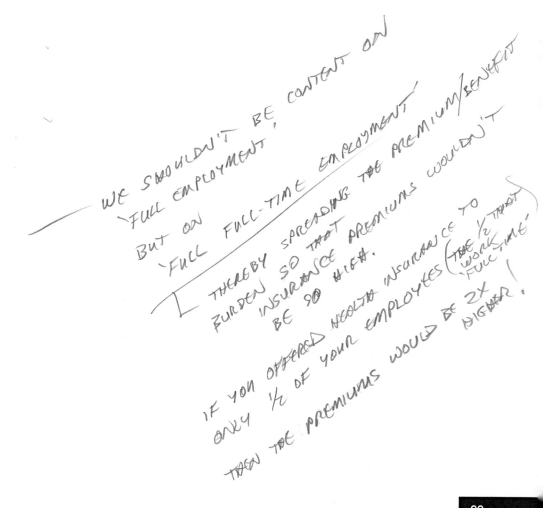

TRAITORS IN OUR CONGRESS

RECENTLY, THE SPEAKER OF THE HOUSE OF REPRESENTATIVES, JOHN Boehner, invited Israeli Prime Minister Benjamin Netanyahu to give an address to a joint session of Congress. This in itself was highly unusual. It is the office of the President that conducts foreign policy. This was the first time the leader of a foreign country had been invited to speak to Congress without first being invited to visit our country by the President. It was yet another in an endless string of attempts to embarrass President Obama and block his initiatives, regardless of merit. Boehner and Netanyahu deliberately timed the visit to undermine the President while he was in the middle of negotiations with Iran—negotiations intended to prevent Iran from developing and arming itself with nuclear weapons.

Even now, there is a standoff with Iran, and geopolitical tensions have increased because of the fear of what the country would do if it had nuclear weapons, and what drastic military actions would have to be taken in response. Israel has made it clear that it is willing to attack Iran to prevent it from developing nuclear weapons. Obviously, this could trigger an all-out

WHY? JUST FOR OIL?
WHAT'S WRONG W/
A NUCLEAR LIMIT W IRAN?

war for the region—which seems to be exactly what Netanyahu wants. The Koch brothers, financing those American politicians who are against an agreement, are of course doing so because they are worried about competition for their oil. Whether an agreement with Iran can be reached remains to be seen. However, after our own recent involvement in two wars in the Middle East, the situation begs for a diplomatic solution. At least we are talking instead of shooting.

However, there is an issue here that is even more important than the threat of war in the Middle East. The fact is that the Speaker of the House of Representatives has deliberately conspired with the leader of a foreign country to undermine the President of the United States. He encouraged the leader of another country to exercise power over the President of the United States. That makes him an outright traitor. He and some other members of Congress are so hell-bent on carrying out their racial prejudice against that "n" word in the White House that they are willing to smear the Office of the Presidency and thereby the reputation of the United States of America in front of the entire world.

The depth of their unrelenting bigotry and their traitorous conduct reminds me of how people like them treated African Americans compared to how they treated German prisoners of war during World War II. Many German POWs were shipped to the United States during the war. They were then placed on trains and taken to POW camps. Some of the camps were located in the south. In those days, when trains coming from the north reached the Mason-Dixon Line, blacks were forced to move to the back of the train because of segregation laws. Because they were white, the German POWs were allowed to stay at the front of the trains. It was as if the southerners were saying, "I'd rather sit beside an enemy of our country, who has probably killed American soldiers, than sit beside an "n" word.

This attitude is fully exemplified by US Senator Tom Cotton, of Arkansas. Cotton drafted a letter that he and forty-nine colleagues signed and sent to the government of Iran. It basically said that negotiations with the President of the United States were meaningless. Keep in mind that these people had no idea what the terms of the agreement could have ended up being. The fact is that they didn't care about the terms of the agreement. Their only concern was preventing that "n" word in the White House from accomplishing or getting credit for anything. Just like in the old days, their racial prejudice was more important to them than even the stature of the presidency. They hate Obama so much that they are willing to undermine and betray everything that the Office of the President of the United States stands for. It is the Office that is important. It is the Office that is described in our Constitution. The Office is far more important than the person holding it. It is the honor and power of the Office that remains after the people holding it are long gone. When you betray the Office, you betray our country.

We all have a right and a duty to criticize the president when he or she is wrong. The Constitution gives us the power to remove an individual from the Office because of misconduct. However, when our own elected officials attack the Office itself because they can't stand the fact that a black man now holds it, they have gone too far. They have become traitors to the Constitution they have taken an oath to uphold. People like Boehner, Cotton, McConnell, and their ilk are remnants of the same history of bigotry and racism that says that certain people should never be truly equal in America, no matter what the Constitution says. It is unfortunate that these racists would rather risk a war in the Middle East than have Obama get credit for preventing one.

ISRAEL, FRIEND OR FOE? IT IS TIME TO RE-EVALUATE

OR DECADES, THE UNITED STATES AND ISRAEL HAVE ENJOYED ONE of the closest alliances of any countries in the world. However, recently that relationship has become so one-sided that Israel is leaving us no choice but to step back and question whether the friendship still exists. This situation is not about Palestine. Most certainly, this is not about anti-Semitism. What this is about is Netanyahu's intentionally and deeply insulting behavior toward our country.

The end run that Netanyahu did around the President to address a joint session of our Congress (as discussed above) was a deep insult. I wonder how the Israelis would feel if President Obama just showed up in Israel, ignored their prime minister, and addressed the Knesset (the equivalent of our Congress). It would be regarded as a slap in the face. Many Knesset members would refuse to attend that address, just like many members of our Congress refused to listen to Netanyahu's.

However, this is not the first time, recently, that Israel's leadership has gone out of its way to publicly embarrass us. In 2010, the United States worked with Israel and Palestine to set up talks designed to help them resolve their territorial disputes. Vice President Biden flew to Israel to facilitate the discussions. Upon his arrival, Biden gave a speech about the long-standing deep friendship and cooperation between our countries.

The very evening before the talks were to begin, Israel announced that it was establishing 1600 new households in a disputed area of the West Bank. There were headlines around the world about how Israel had humiliated Biden and the United States. The issue is not that Israel established the households. The issue is that they waited until we arrived, and then rubbed it in our faces. They could have at least waited until after the talks had concluded. Instead, they went out of their way to smack us in the face. This is not how you treat your closest, most powerful, and (let's be honest) only true ally in the world. President Obama should have ordered Biden back home, and retaliated against Israel in some significant way, immediately. Any country that intentionally tries to humiliate us in front of the whole world is not our friend.

Since World War II, the US has given more foreign aid to Israel than to any other country—a total of $121 billion (currently $3 billion per year), most of it in the form of military aid. We just gave over $400 million to help them pay for their most advanced missile defense system yet. Even though Israel is hardly a poor, underdeveloped country, I have no problem with all of this financial support, because I am a strong supporter of Israel.

The reasons for that support go back as far as my earliest childhood. Many people know about the bombing of the African American church in Birmingham, Alabama—an act of violence that killed four little girls during the early days of the civil rights movement. Fewer people have heard about the bombing of the synagogue that occurred in Atlanta when I was growing up there in the 1950s. That may be because (fortunately) no one was killed. I did not understand why this "church" was bombed, because the people who went there were white. My mother explained to me that many people hated Jews because of their religious beliefs. One summer when I was still in grade school, my mother and I traveled by car with another family for a vacation to Florida. In the days of racial segregation, we could not sit down and eat in white restaurants. Some of them would allow blacks to go around to the back door, or to a side window to order food. We stopped at such a place for lunch. The owner apologized for not allowing us to come in and sit down. He said that he was Jewish, and that "they" hated Jews almost as much as they hated us. He said that if he allowed us to come in, his place would be burned down by the next morning.

There are many experiences that cause a bond to be formed between people. One of them is the common experience of discrimination and persecution. Some of the kinship I feel toward Jews comes from the fact that when I was a child, many of the Freedom Riders who came from the north to join us in our fight for equality and our civil rights were Jewish. They voluntarily put their personal safety and lives on the line for our cause. Andrew Goodman and Michael Schwerner—two of the three Freedom Riders who were murdered in Mississippi—were Jewish. The other was James Chaney, an African American. It was not until I got to college that I began to understand the centuries upon centuries of persecution that Jews had to endure in just about every country they lived in, culminating in modern times with the Holocaust.

There is an exhibit of photographs of black people who had been lynched by murderous bigots in the south. The horror of it brings to the surface every one of the worst feelings and emotions about the limitless injustice, degradation, and cruelty suffered by African Americans in this country. The pain of it overwhelms your very core. However, even this pales when you try to imagine the relentless systematic murder of six million people by the Nazis. If they could have, they would have killed every Jew in the world. I do not believe anyone could experience the Holocaust Museum in Washington D. C. and not be a supporter of Israel and their motto of "Never Again." So anyone who interprets my position on the present state of US-Israel relations as prejudice against Jews or as anti-Israel, tell it to somebody else. The truth is that Benjamin Netanyahu and John Boehner put their personal political ambitions above the strong partnership between our countries.

The deal that they cut with each other is obvious. Boehner would help Netanyahu get re-elected if Netanyahu would help the Republicans in Congress get more of the Jewish vote, and more Jewish political money. The Jewish lobby in support of Israel is one of the most well-financed in Washington. Netanyahu had the unmitigated gall to stand up before Congress and say that his visit was not political, even though his re-election bid in Israel was only two weeks away. He obviously thinks that Congress and the American people are too stupid to realize that his speech was meant to get votes in Israel. Of course, Boehner was more than willing to demean the stature of Congress by allowing it to be used as a tool for Netanyahu's re-election. Someone needs to remind him that Netanyahu is the prime minister of Israel, not prime minister of the United States. He is obviously free to take any position he wants regarding US foreign policy. However, he has rudely and arrogantly injected himself into the internal affairs of our government. That cannot be tolerated any more than Israel would tolerate it if the situation were reversed. As for Boehner, since he has more loyalty to the prime minister of Israel than to the President of the United States, he should relinquish his US citizenship and move to Israel. Netanyahu would certainly find him a good job to repay his betrayal of his former country.

Netanyahu may have won his election, but in doing so, he

damaged the friendship between our countries. When someone like myself who supports Israel finds it necessary to consider withdrawing that support, I know that I am not alone. I suspect that many Jewish Americans were disturbed by his willingness to risk destabilizing the longstanding, strategically important friendship between our countries. Like the rest of us, American Jews are Americans, first. None of us like to see the United States embarrassed by any foreign leader. Especially considering that President Obama received sixty-nine percent of the Jewish vote in 2012. This overwhelming support obviously means nothing to Netanyahu. Nor does it seem to matter to him that Obama has that kind of support partly because American Jews consider him to be a true friend of Israel. As an African American, I must conclude that Netanyahu is well aware that most of the political opposition to President Obama is racially motivated. Netanyahu has not treated any other US President with the disrespect that he has shown to President Obama. My conclusion is that he shares the racist attitudes of many in our Congress. Undoubtedly, he used their racism toward Obama to help get himself re-elected.

However, despite all of the issues above, the most offensive thing about Netanyahu's insults to our country is that he does not seem to understand that much if not most of the radical Islamic animosity and hatred of the United States is because of our friendship with Israel. I want the US to stand by Israel, regardless. However, we should only pay the price of radical Islamic hatred if our alliance and friendship is true.

With respect to Palestine, it is no secret that Israel continues to annex more and more of the disputed territory. Why shouldn't they? They have been under attack since their country was founded. They are surrounded by countries that have vowed to destroy them. They have won every war against their enemies. Many attempts at negotiating peace have fallen apart. They have the most powerful military in the region. Why should they behave any differently than any other country that has the advantage over their enemies?

At the risk of being naive and simplistic, I come back to my image of the Jews who stood with us during the civil rights movement because they understood our plight because of the unimaginable discrimination that Jews have experienced. I believe that those of us who have experienced discrimination and persecution have a special responsibility to stand up against it whenever we can. Abraham Lincoln could have allowed retribution against the South. Nelson Mandela could have justifiably sought retribution against the white South Africans who repressed his people under apartheid. But if these great men had done so, there would have been one cycle of violence after another.

My observation is that Israel's leadership is treating the Palestinians more and more like oppressors and persecutors have treated Jews over the years. If it continues, we know how it will eventually end. All of human history and most certainly the history of Jews shows that the oppressed will eventually fight back and find some way to cast off their oppressors. It is my sincere belief that the evil experienced by their ancestors will cause the people of Israel to express humanity and fairness toward the Palestinians, because discrimination and cruelty only begets more hatred and violence. Israel not only has the power to protect itself—it also has the power to be a force for peace in the Middle East and the world. As a country that was born out of the most inhumane possible treatment of its people, Israel could set an example for the world by seeking peace, tolerance, and mutual benefit with the Palestinians. Right now, under Netanyahu, it is doing just the opposite.

THE PUPPET MASTERS

ACCORDING TO THE CENTER FOR MEDIA AND DEMOCRACY,

The Tea Party itself is not a political party; it is a conglomerate of loosely affiliated "grassroots" organizations such as the Tea Party Nation, Tea Party Patriots, Tax Day Tea Party, and others. While the Movement has no formal political affiliations, many members endorse Republican candidates for office. There is also a Tea Party Caucus in the United States Congress. Although the Tea Party has no official platform, most of the groups associated with the Movement share the same basic ideological position on domestic and foreign affairs in that they are anti-government, anti-spending, anti-immigration, and anti-compromise politics. While promoted as a spontaneous "grassroots" movement, many of the activities of Tea Party groups were organized by corporate lobbying groups like Freedomworks and Americans for Prosperity.[15]

KOCH FOUNDED

Promote 'American Dream' of the Rich on the Taxation of the poor.

a variety of 'deficit' spending

The founder of Americans for Prosperity was none other than David Koch of the Koch brothers, who has given millions to the Tea Party and other conservative causes. Their agenda opposes federal deficits, has no objection to giving trillions in tax cuts to corporations and the superrich, opposes the extension of unemployment benefits, and opposes an increase in the minimum wage. According to Jane Mayer, who in 2010 did an in-depth report on the Koch brothers for the *New Yorker*, the role of Americans for Prosperity was to help educate Tea Party activists and provide funding and organization.[16] The Koch brothers, with a web of deceit and manipulation, pulled in unsuspecting Americans who were mad as hell as the economy slammed into their American dream. They also played the race card, taking full advantage of the backlash of racism caused by the election of the first African American President. Obviously, they share this racism, given their long-standing opposition to civil rights. These Americans were ripe for the picking and the Koch brothers took advantage of the timing to turn us against each other so we wouldn't look their way.

Tea Party members, like many Republicans, are anti-government—at least when it comes to taxes, business, and social programs. They claim government is the root of all evil. They hate regulations, and also handouts to the less fortunate. As activist CJ Ferry recently put it, the Tea Party is the "voice of that anger."

Though I am digressing, I think it important to note that *we* are the Government. Whatever it does, it does in our name. When a child gets maimed in an industrial accident, we cry for regulation to protect our children. When business monopolies artificially raise prices, we scream for price regulation and/or the breakup of monopolies. When a child or an unwanted elderly person is found homeless, hungry, or abused, we cry for the protection of our most vulnerable. When a neighbor pollutes our rivers, affecting our drinking water, we are up in arms for regulation. Our government is a direct result of We the People coming together to provide and care for our children and communities. We create laws and regulations to help us live in a democracy, protecting our individual rights and freedom, but balancing that with the protection and needs of our society as a whole. It isn't easy, folks, but it's the best there is. How can we deny that we are responsible? Even when we tune out and drop out and allow the rich to take over our government, we are responsible.

Also, let me say this, as emphatically as possible, to Tea Party members in general. I believe I speak for most Americans when I say that if we could put up with eight years of George W. Bush running the economy into the ground and getting us into two unnecessary wars, you sure as hell can work with Barack Obama! Get over it, like we had to. He was our President whether we liked it or not. Regardless of how Republican Tea Party members in Congress feel about the President personally, the people have elected him twice. These politicians have an obligation to work with him in good faith out of respect for the office of the President—and, more importantly, out of respect for the people. If they can't bring themselves to do that, then they should resign. The point is that our government is not about the President, members of Congress, or obscene amounts of money. It is about We the People and our great country. To some politicians, both have become irrelevant. The only thing that matters to them is the game of politics, money, and their prejudice. The only power that is strong enough to overcome their obsession is the power granted to each and every American: our vote. The founders of our country, in their wisdom, gave us the last say. The time has come for us to use it to get our country back where it should be, which is getting better and better, and greater and greater, and stronger and stronger. Are you a Great American? Please be one: our country needs you. VOTE!

DISDAIN EVEN FOR OUR SOLDIERS

I NEVER THOUGHT THAT I WOULD SEE THE DAY THAT REPUBLICANS would abandon their support for our soldiers, especially in times of war. Over the years, they have constantly bashed Democrats for being weak on national defense. However, the mean spirit of the Tea Party Republicans in Congress knows no bounds. As I write, health care for the military and their families is being cut back because of the "sequester," and our "leaders" (in name only) are once again showing that they could care less. How do you think that affects the morale of our soldiers—particularly our combat soldiers, who are putting it all on the line for us? There is even talk of cutting their pay. They are weakening our military at a time when China is rapidly and aggressively building up its military, and Russia, under Vladimir Putin, is falling back into its Cold War mentality. These very same Republicans have always been quick to invoke the name of President Ronald Reagan to justify themselves. President Reagan was unswerving in his belief in and support for a strong military. That is what brought the Cold War to an end. President Reagan would be appalled by the weakening of our military, and in total disbelief that it was being done by his own party. I also think he would be angered by the shabby treatment of military personnel who have been injured serving our country.

There is no limit to the arrogance and disrespect that these people have towards the American people, except for the super-rich plutocrats that they are willing to do anything for. When they mistreat the people who protect our country and us, our government has gone terribly wrong. They must be voted out. They will ignore the sacrifices of our soldiers and weaken our country until we do. ARE YOU A GREAT AMERICAN?

Many of our elected officials have sided with and adopted the attitude of the would-be kings and queens of America, that their money makes them better than the rest of us—even the people who fight and die for us and them. MFA, if it were not for the ultimate sacrifices made by our military, these egomaniacs would not have a country to be super-rich in, and they wouldn't have the profits that many of them make from war. In 2011 the Commission on Wartime Contracting estimated that $177 billion had been spent in the previous decade on private contracts in Afghanistan and Iraq. From the Revolutionary War to Afghanistan, it is the "average" American, not the elitist, who has fought and suffered and died so that there could be a United States of America.

MFA, we cannot allow ourselves or our government to be hypocrites when it comes to our military. We cannot claim to be patriotic Americans and at the same time stand by and allow the people who protect us and our country to be treated with such disrespect. While it is all-but-impossible for us to comprehend what our combat soldiers go through, we must acknowledge as best we can their courage, and the ultimate sacrifice that they make for our country. No combat veteran should get less than the best treatment for his or her physical and mental injuries. Needless to say, none of them should be homeless—even though many of them are. The President, Congress, and the American people should be ashamed of the backlog of veterans who have been waiting months and even years to receive the benefits that are due to them from the Veterans Administration. Stacks and stacks of claims and records are not even computerized. This cannot be how Americans treat their heroes. We the people must stand up to our government for them, and for their families, who are suffering right along with them. ARE YOU A GREAT AMERICAN?

DISGRACE IN THE RANKS OF OUR BEST

THERE ARE MANY THINGS THAT DEFINE THE GREATNESS OF OUR country. However, the characteristic that truly distinguishes us from the rest of the world is the will of the American people to embrace the ideal of freedom, fairness, and opportunity for all of its citizens, regardless of background. Even though discrimination against many Americans still prevails, there is no question that we are pursuing the best idea ever conceived by and for humanity. However, in the face of this progress there are acts of discrimination that are so heinous and contrary to our values as to make them almost unbelievable.

Like other victims of discrimination, women have made great strides towards equality. Yet that discrimination stubbornly lingers, especially considering that women make up half of our population; are not a "minority"; are mostly white and have the power of half of the country's votes.

However, when we look at what is happening to women in our military, discrimination has taken the form of one of the most serious crimes in our society other than murder. The US Department of Defense estimates that in 2012, over 12,000 sexual assaults against servicewomen occurred in our military. That is an average of thirty-three per day. Sexual assault is defined as rape, non-consensual sodomy, or abusive sexual conduct. Sexual harassment is not included in the definition. Other estimates indicate that one in five service women are sexually assaulted. The head of the program to prevent sexual assaults in the US Air Force was himself recently charged with sexual assault. West Point, the Naval Academy, and the Air Force Academy have all been rocked by scandals in which widespread sexual assaults against women cadets had been covered up. Of those who actually reported sexual assaults, more than half said that they were retaliated against for doing so. Only three out of a hundred reported sexual assaults are ever prosecuted in the military.

I am not a veteran, but like so many Americans I not only support our military, I have a deep reverence and gratitude for their service and sacrifice. When these sexual assaults surfaced, for me it was a "please don't let it be true" moment. It would be naive to think that our military is immune from the problems experienced by our society in general. What is disturbing and disappointing about the military situation is that hardly anything is being done about it. Few cases are even prosecuted, let alone perpetrators punished. Often the servicewoman is re-victimized for reporting what happened.

From the days of slavery through most of the years of racial segregation in the south, men—especially white men—raped black women with impunity. That is why so few African-Americans actually look like pure Africans today. It most certainly wasn't because of black men having sex with white women. In those days, that was the equivalent of a black man committing suicide. African-American women not only had to endure the degradation and humiliation of being owned or discriminated against—they also suffered the ultimate mental and physical violation of their persons and nobody did anything about it.

Now women of all backgrounds are being sexually assaulted in our military, which of course, is part of the United States government. The 2014 Documentary, *The Invisible War*, indicates that among all active-duty female soldiers, twenty percent are sexually assaulted.[17] We know it—and have known it for a long time—and still nothing has been done to stop it. In fact, incredibly, the situation is getting worse. In this day and age, how can this be? This is serious criminal conduct that is no more representative of our military personnel than it is for most of us in civilian life. Please watch this documentary and hear from the women who have actually experienced this outrage.

Perhaps the problem is mine, in that I have set a standard of military conduct that is too high. When I think of our military, I think of courageous, skilled warriors, with the highest sense of duty. But I also think of warriors with the highest sense of honor. It is my hope that our military will not only stop these heinous crimes within its ranks, but will set the example for our entire country that there is zero tolerance for this type of conduct toward women, whether in military or civilian life. In the past several years, 89,000 cases of rape per year have been reported in the United States. The actual number is no doubt much higher. The command structure is at the core of military effectiveness. However, to solve this problem there must be prosecutorial independence, within the military, that will handle these serious crimes impartially through the due process of law. Our military should do this voluntarily, to demonstrate our genuine concern for the treatment of women. However, if it won't, the President as Commander-in-Chief and the Congress should act immediately to stop these crimes—even if it means prosecuting the cases outside of the military justice system. If necessary, we must force them to take action with our voices and votes.

Unfortunately, it's not just the military that tolerates the sexual abuse of women. Statistics indicate that one in five college women are sexually assaulted. In *The Hunting Ground*, one of the films at the 2015 Sundance Film Festival, it is revealed that there is an endemic system of institutional cover-ups, rationalizations, victim blaming, and denial in US colleges and universities when it comes to the rape of women. Our college campuses are supposed to be places where students are able to grow and learn in an atmosphere of freedom and safety. Women students should not have to live in fear of sexual predators.

I recently read that every day in America, at least four women are murdered by a domestic partner. Thirty-five percent of all emergency room calls are the result of domestic violence. And a new investigation by USA Today reports that over 70,000 rape kits in America aren't even being processed. My fellow Americans, where is our outrage? Where is the anger that propels us to act to protect our own? We should be ashamed. Any time you hear someone lamenting about the women living under terrorist rule in the Middle East, stop and think about what we are allowing to happen to women in our own country. This must stop! ARE YOU A GREAT AMERICAN?

LAST FRONTIER OF THE CIVIL RIGHTS MOVEMENT: EQUAL RIGHTS FOR WOMEN

WHETHER IT IS THE ISSUE OF EQUAL PAY FOR EQUAL WORK, STOPPING the rape and sexual abuse of women in the military and on campuses, or some other issue, women have the political clout to change it for the better.

One of my true heroes is former Congresswoman Shirley Chisholm. She represented a district in Brooklyn, New York for many years, and was the second woman to run for President. She was quoted as saying that in America she would be free as a black person before she would be free as a woman. There was a time when I would have disagreed with her because it was inconceivable to me that a white person of either gender would be mistreated more than us. As they used to say, "If you're white, you're right; if you're black, get back." Now I have come to understand that she was right.

In the past, when discrimination was most blatant, it was aimed at us "minorities." As the civil rights movement progresses and the American people increasingly reject blatantly unfair treatment, we are now left to confront the effects of less obvious, more insidious forms of discrimination.

Obviously, gay Americans have been waging a long, extremely difficult battle against some of the most deep-seated prejudices in our society. As with other civil rights movements, progress has been slow, and there is a long way before we reach true equality and fair treatment. Yet real progress is being made, especially lately.

The reasons for this progress are the same as the other civil rights movements. Gay Americans have made it absolutely clear to politicians that they are politically active and that they vote. Also, as with others of us, they have stood up at defining moments and said, "We are not asking, we are demanding our full rights as Americans." Such a moment occurred in 1969, at the Stonewall Inn in New York City, where gay people took a stand against continual harassment by the police. After numerous police raids, and being hauled off to jail, the patrons of the Inn stood against this unfair treatment and oppression, by saying, "No more!" Three days of rioting made it clear that they would not take anymore. That stand began to change the course of their future. Now look at how many politicians who were vehemently opposed to gay marriage have suddenly "seen the light" and have reversed their positions. This is the mighty power of political involvement and the vote.

Again, however, we are talking about the struggle for equal rights by people who are a fraction of a country's population. I cannot help but try to imagine what the African American civil rights movement would be like if we were half the population, like women, and had that many votes. It is a great reservoir of political power that is often unused. I do not in any way assert that women are or should be monolithic in their thinking or opinions on any given issue. However, it is a long-standing unfortunate fact that women are singled out for unfair treatment simply and only because they are women. The only question is what are women and the rest of us going to do about it? How can we say our country stands for freedom, fairness, and opportunity, if half of its population is discriminated against? Women have half of the nation's political clout to stop it and all Americans should stand with them.

There are issues that affect almost all women, regardless of politics. How can it be that in this day and age, women with the same or better qualifications make seventy-seven percent of the pay of men, for doing exactly the same work? African Americans started out in this country as slaves, making no money at all. Even we have made serious progress toward equal pay. I have no doubt that if enough women seriously demanded that Congress pass laws that women must receive equal pay for equal work it would happen right now. But Congress is ignoring you. Even during the 2015 State of the Union, when President Obama called for equal pay for women, most Republicans, including female Republican senators and representatives, sat on their hands as others applauded. They dismissed the issue as unimportant. I wonder how those Republican congresswomen would feel if their paychecks were twenty-three percent less than their male counterparts.

They will continue to ignore you until you stand up and vote them out. By the way, don't listen to that garbage about how women will be hurt—the false argument that if you increase women's pay, more women will be laid off. The more money people make, the more they spend, and the more the economy expands, creating even more jobs. Imagine what would happen to the economy if men's pay were suddenly cut by twenty-three percent. It would all but collapse. The key is investing more in education and training for men and women so everyone can make more money.

The controversial issue that is certainly unique for women is that of reproductive rights. Obviously, women disagree strongly about this issue. Nevertheless, most women believe that it is their choice whether or not to have a child. Many seem to be unaware that there is a serious, relentless, well-fi-nanced campaign to take that choice away, regardless of cir-cumstance. Not surprisingly, this campaign is led mostly by men. Do not assume that they can't succeed. We have a Con-gress that has sold out the entire middle class of both genders and a Supreme Court with five Catholic men who have openly displayed their disdain for a woman's right to choose. These are politicians who are not even pretending to be fair. If they sense that women are so complacent as to let them get away with it, it could happen tomorrow.

As with other groups who are struggling for fairness and equality, this is not just about women. It is about all of us and the well-being of our country. My father and mother were divorced when I was five years old. I never saw my father again, and he provided no financial assistance to my mother and me. If my mother had not had the incredible fortitude to become a nurse at a time when very few blacks were even allowed to get an education, let alone become professionals, we would have lived in poverty. As it was, she was deliberately underpaid because she was black and because she was a woman. She sac-rificed everything to educate me. As she said the first time we discussed the issue of women's liberation, "Son, I was liberated whether I wanted to be or not." Every opportunity that I have had to make something of myself I owe to her.

Today, as before, there are millions of children and young people whose sole means of support are their mothers. Yet after all these years, most of these women are still underpaid, and the impact is felt acutely by their children. Half of the children of single mothers live below the poverty line. How long is this going to be allowed to continue? If we tell lawmakers that we will vote them out if they don't make the changes, and if they know that we really mean it, you can take that to the bank. Like the LGBT community, which is feared and respected because they are politically active and they vote, women and middle class Americans must use their votes to demand respect and change our country for the better.

THE ANGRY WHITE MAN

ONE OF THE BIASES OF OUR SOCIETY IS THAT WHITE MEN ARE ALLOWED to be angry. If a black man becomes angry, he is labeled with the ugly stereotype of "the angry black man." People use that term constantly. They either don't know or don't care that what they are saying is that it's okay for a white man to be angry, but it's not okay for a black man. Why is that? I guess we're supposed to be grinning all the time. Maybe we should do some shuffling while we're at it. When a white man is angry, he is being "strong" and "forceful." When a black man is angry, he is being "unseemly," "uppity," and "out of his place." While we're at it, we may as well bring the "pushy woman" into the discussion. Women are not allowed to be angry or strong without being stereotyped as well. But I know that if my mother had not been strong and sometimes angry, she would not have achieved the amazing things that she did with her life in the racist, sexist South—including raising me as a single parent.

Personally, I have found that carrying anger around is bad for me physically and mentally, especially now that I am older.

But don't tell me that it's okay for a white man to be angry and it isn't okay for me. That will make me angry for sure.

It is no secret that some white men are angry because the people elected a black man as president. There was a sharp rise in hate crimes after President Obama was elected, and suddenly everybody appeared to be buying guns and ammunition. Again, that is no surprise, especially when you have hate-mongers like the Koch brothers, who spend millions of dollars appealing to people's racial prejudices in order to destroy Obama's presidency and distract us from their attempt to take over our government and economically exploit all middle-class Americans, including white people. Remember, the biggest losers from the financial crisis are white men. Why aren't you angry with the greedy, arrogant white men on Wall Street—the ones who caused the economy to melt down? Why aren't you angry with the Koch brothers, and their buddies who are doing everything that they can to turn the middle class into the working poor? Is it because they are white men?

If you don't think that white people aren't suffering in ways that only used to happen to us underprivileged "minorities," look at the facts. Between 1999 and 2013, white Americans between the ages of 45 to 54 began dying at a sharply increased rate, while the death rate for every other age group, race, and ethnicity actually declined, according to a study by two Princeton economists (one of whom, Angus Deaton, was awarded the 2015 Nobel Prize in Economics[18]). The main causes of death were not the usual things that kill so many Americans, such as diabetes and heart disease. Instead, the main causes of death were suicide, substance abuse, alcoholic liver disease, and overdoses of heroin and prescription opiates. Such statistics are sad and tragic, regardless of the background of the Americans involved. However, this report is especially sobering because white people are hardly ever at the bottom when it comes to issues of poor health. Until now, African Americans have usually occupied that space.

You don't have to be a mental-health professional or scientist to see that these deaths are the result of severe stress. And there can be no doubt that most of this stress was brought about by these Americans' inability to make a decent living—a direct result of the financial crisis. The Wall Street bankers' greed-fest all but destroyed the economy, and these Americans were the least able to cope. Instead of taking action to improve the economy and create jobs, the angry white Republicans in Congress blocked every attempt by the Obama administration to stimulate the economy. Their main goal was to defeat Obama every time, and at all cost—rather than helping the American people recover from financial disaster. Assisted by most Republican governors, these angry white men did everything they could to destroy or block ObamaCare. It was more important for them to smack Obama than to provide lifesaving healthcare for their people.

I don't care if you're angry, racially prejudiced, or an outright bigot. Just don't be fools for the elitists who are abusing all of us as cheap labor so they can make more money. They are manipulating you to do their dirty work against your own self-interest.

ECONOMIC DEMOCRACY: VOTE WITH YOUR DOLLARS

Every American has a type of vote that is just as powerful as going to the polls. We use it every single day: our money. We must never forget that we vote every time that we buy something.

Earlier, I mentioned how the CEO of Chick-fil-A spoke out publicly and unequivocally against gay marriage. Recently, he made a "clarifying statement" that all are welcome in his restaurants. Why did he find it necessary to backpedal? Because he had become concerned about how his original statement would affect his business.

Not long ago, Target, the department store chain, made a financial contribution to an organization that opposed the gay rights movement. After an uproar from many of Target's employees and customers, Target CEO Gregg Steinhofel admitted his mistake. CEOs of some other companies took note. Then they prevailed upon their stooges in Congress and on the US Supreme Court to give them a way to hide their right-wing political activities from their customers and employees. There were two results: super PACs from our bought-and-paid-for Congress, and the Citizens United decision from the five Supreme

Court in-justices who said that Americans have no right to know where the people we elect get their money from.

The companies and businesses in our competitive free enterprise system are like our Aladdin's Lamps. Our wishes are their commands. They must have our money or they perish. If you go into a store and get mistreated, you stop shopping there and go somewhere else. Competition is one of the greatest things about free enterprise. There is always another business to buy from. That is why the largest and most powerful multinational corporations can be shaken to their foundations by one simple word: boycott. This is why some companies and their CEOs want to hide like cowards behind Super PACs and try to take over our government without us knowing it.

Such companies want to hurt their customers and still take their money. This is no different from the situation that launched the black civil rights movement. The City of Montgomery, Alabama wanted to treat blacks like dirt by making them ride in the back of the bus, while still taking the money they paid for each ticket. Rosa Parks said, "No more," and the rest, as they say, is history. It was a boycott of the bus system that ended segregation on the buses, and led to the rise of the civil rights movement and Dr. Martin Luther King, Jr. This is true even though, at the time, most black people had no other means of transportation.

More recently, homophobic members of the Arizona Legislature passed a bill that allowed merchants to refuse service to gay Americans. The Governor vetoed the bill—mainly because its implementation would have resulted in a financial disaster for the state, due to boycotts by individuals and organizations refusing to do business or hold events in the state. In this case, the threat of financial loss defeated discrimination. The threat of financial loss will also stop these elitists and their companies from abusing the middle class.

If politicians treat us with disrespect at the behest of some elitist plutocrats, we must use our ballots to vote them out. However, it is just as important to use the power of our money to stop buying from or doing business with people who treat us as their peons. Of course, this presupposes that we care enough to be watchful and hold them accountable. Are you a Great American?

I'M A DEMOCRAT—WHERE THE (BLEEP) IS MY PARTY?

I AM A DEMOCRAT BECAUSE IT IS THE PARTY THAT HAS STOOD UP FOR Americans who were being treated unfairly. It protected working people from being exploited by the rich and powerful. It has fought against discrimination and supported every group that has had to struggle for its rights. I will never forget President Lyndon Baines Johnson saying the words, "We shall overcome," and signing the Voting Rights Act. I held public office as a Democrat for eighteen years. It is difficult to describe how deeply it saddens me now to say that I have no idea what my party stands for, and to wonder what has happened to our backbone.

Even when we've had majorities in the House and Senate of the Congress, we've been on the defensive. The general tone for Democrats seems to be to keep quiet, keep your head down, and don't make waves—while the Republican Tea Party runs amuck and attacks everything we used to stand for. The Republicans in our Congress have allowed themselves to be taken over by the bomb-throwing loonies in the Tea Party. At the same time, the Democrats have become what I call the "T & T Party"—the party of the timid and tepid.

BESIDES CIVIL RIGHTS + WELFARE

It is not enough for Democrats to say, "At least we are not crazy and ridiculous like the Tea-Party Republicans." We have to stand for something, sharply contrasting ourselves with them. We have to lead instead of standing quietly by and acquiescing to their ultra-right-wing madness. Slowly but surely, the American middle class is coming to realize that we are being shamelessly abused by some of the rich and powerful, who are using their money to grind us into serfdom. As I mentioned at the outset of this book, it is now official. For the first time, the United States of America no longer has the richest middle class in the world. We have been surpassed by Canada—and other nations are poised to surpass us soon too if our government continues to treat us like servants, instead of serving and investing in us. While most of the elitists who seem to despise the middle class are aligned with the Republican Tea Party, many Democrats take their money as well, and are doing nothing to protect us from them. If you won't stand up for us, what good are you? You need to be voted out also.

More and more rank-and-file Republicans and Democrats are coming to realize that their elected officials, especially in Congress, are so preoccupied with raising campaign money—and appeasing the rich and powerful who have it—that the rest of us don't count. As people suffer more as a result of being ignored, we will come to care enough to hold the offending elected officials accountable and throw them out regardless of party. Even rank-and-file Tea Party members are coming to realize that their representatives in Congress are selling them out. One issue where there is common ground among the rank and file of each party is resentment at the destruction of our livelihoods by the big Wall Street banks. Yet the Tea Party members in Congress are taking their money and sucking up to them, just like the Republicans and Democrats. Vote them out. ARE YOU A GREAT AMERICAN?

THE KOCHING OF AMERICA

At this time, our country is actually living out George Orwell's book, *Animal Farm*. For those who haven't read it, the Koch brothers and their ilk are the elitist pigs. The American middle class is the workhorse that the pigs eventually work to death and send to the glue factory.

MFAs, we must learn from our past. We've been here before, and we will be here again until we learn. In 1934, the *New York Times* ran an article about an alleged plot to overthrow the United States Government; this plot was exposed by Major General Smedley D. Butler in testimony before a Congressional committee. David Woolner, historian for the Franklin and Eleanor Roosevelt Institute, reports that

> according to Butler, a group of wealthy individuals, many of whom worked on Wall Street, had asked him to lead a 500,000 strong march of ex-servicemen on Washington with the intent of bringing down FDR and establishing a fascist regime.

This was treason! Woolner goes on to say:

> A few months before the business plot came to light, for example, a group of prominent public officials and wealthy businessmen formed an organization called the American Liberty League. Billed as a research and opinion organization, the Liberty League's primary focus was to attack FDR and the New Deal. Accusing the president and his recovery programs of being—at various times—fascistic, socialistic or communistic, the real goal of the League was to return the country to the rule of unfettered and unregulated free enterprise a la the 1920s.

Sound familiar? Woolner continues:

> Characterizing the League as a tool of what he called "selfish big business," FDR would go on to remind the public that the wealthy interests behind such groups tended "to consider the Government of the United States as a mere appendage to their own affairs." Indeed, based on the experience of the late 20s and early 30s, he continued, we "know now that Government by organized money is just as dangerous as Government by organized mob."[19]

The American people saw through the ruse and re-elected FDR by a landslide. The Liberty League faded away, as such movements often do, until new extremists like the Koch brothers came along to try once again to control America through smoke-and-mirrors and unlimited pocketbooks.

If you don't know who Charles and David Koch are, you should. They want to be our Kings. Not President of the United States, but the Kings of the United States of America. How can that be? The United States is a democracy, not a monarchy. But the Kochs' approach is really very simple: instead of being elected as head of our government, you just flat out buy the government. All you have to do is have enough money—but this is no problem for the Koch brothers. They are multi-billionaires. Yet there is one difference between these brothers and other monarchs. They want to be "Secret Kings." They want to be our Kings without us even knowing about it. They must be very shy. To be "Secret Kings," however, you have to secretly buy the government, because people might get upset if they realized that they were being taken over without their consent.

What they did for years was create and support front organizations that would hide what the secret money was really for. They have un-kingly names like Americans for Prosperity, Citizens for a Sound Economy, FreedomWorks, and the Federalist Society. Then they contacted other would-be "secret kings" (i.e., other billionaires and large corporations) to help pay for the secret takeover of our democracy.

Of course, the "secret kings" must have servants. No problem there—all they have to do is buy the servants that We the People (hereinafter, nobodies) elected, and have them serve them instead of us. *We can buy them on the cheap,* they think. *They will sell their souls to get elected. For a few thousand dollars we can own most of them. The rest will be so intimidated and afraid of us and our vast amounts of secret money that they will keep their mouths shut and go along with whatever we want.*

What about the nobodies? Won't they be mad at us taking them over and making them poorer and poorer? Not to worry. They don't care enough to pay attention to what their elected officials are doing to them. They're like sheep. All we have to do is use our secret money to throw a few sound bites to them at election time. They won't even notice that the people they elected now work for us instead of them.

Besides, now that we have that "n" word as president, all we have to do is tap into their prejudices and fears. They will be so busy hating him that they won't notice that we are getting richer and causing them to be poorer. The old "divide and conquer" works every time. We have so much secret money that we can form our own party to whip them up and channel all of that fear, bigotry, and anger to serve our own purposes. Let's call it the Tea Party. We can pay people to go around the country to attack him and every idea of his. They will be so busy going after him that they won't notice that we have no respect for them either, and that our goal is to become richer by exploiting all of them and making them the working poor. We can actually manipulate them into doing our dirty work against Obama and even themselves. Perfect . . .

Each Koch brother (Charles and David) is worth more than $40 billion dollars. Koch touts one financial figure of $115 billion in annual revenue—mostly from petroleum products. They lease many of the tar-sands in Alberta and are pushing for the Keystone Pipeline. They counted on politicians to do their bidding to increase their profit and invisible power. It is not a coincidence that the number one priority of the Republican agenda in Congress after the 2014 election has been the passage of the bill authorizing the Keystone Pipeline—even though there is currently a glut of oil on the world market and this pipeline will help the Canadian petroleum industry compete against the United States producers for market share in an increasingly competitive environment. In the end, the goal is profit for the Koch brothers, in return for the hundreds of millions that they contribute to political campaigns. In November 2015, President Obama foiled their efforts by vetoing the Keystone Pipeline bill, stating that after careful study, the State Department ruled that the Keystone Pipeline "would not serve the national interest of the United States."

The Koch brothers also own Georgia Pacific, which sells plywood to Home Depot, and also owns brand names like Dixie Cups, Brawny Paper towels, Stainmaster Carpet, and Angel Soft toilet paper. In 2013 Koch jumped into high technology and bought Molex, a manufacturer of electronic components, and a top supplier to smartphone makers, including Apple. In the Chapter "Vote with your Dollars," I pointed out how Chick-fil-A and Target were shamed into supporting equal rights by their customers and employees. It was a business decision. The point was that people should not spend their hard-earned money supporting businesses that discriminate against them. If you oppose the "Koching of America," you should vote with your dollars. Make your money count twice. The Koch brother's wealth was passed down from their father and yet the Koch brothers are against the minimum wage, saying that it "creates a culture of dependency." Really? These boys, who started out with money inherited from their father, make $1.8 million every hour. Much of it comes from polluting our land, rivers, and skies. They were slapped with what was then the largest fine ever: $30 million, for over 300 oil spills.

Fred Koch, the father of Charles and David, built his fortune from working with none other than Joseph Stalin, the former dictator of the Soviet Union. According to Tim Dickinson, writing in *Rolling Stone,*

> With his domestic business tied up in court, Fred started looking for partners abroad and was soon doing business in the Soviet Union, where leader Joseph Stalin had just launched his first Five Year Plan. Stalin sought to fund his country's industrialization by selling oil into the lucrative European export market. But the Soviet Union's reserves were notoriously hard to refine. The USSR needed cracking technology and the Oil Directorate of the Supreme Council on the National Economy took a shining to Winkler-Koch—primarily

because Koch's oil-industry competitors were reluctant to do business with totalitarian Communists.[20]

During the time Koch helped the USSR's industrial revolution, Stalin's Great Purge killed at least 20 million people. Fred remained focused on making money until his distaste for Communism brought him home.

Similar to their father, profit comes first. The Koch brothers worked with those on the "do not fly list" to undermine America's position against Terrorists in Iran. According to *Rolling Stone* magazine,

> In the years after George W. Bush branded Iran a member of the 'Axis of Evil,' the Koch brothers profited from trade with Iran. For decades, US companies have been forbidden from doing business with the Ayatollahs, but Koch Industries exploited a loophole in the 1996 sanctions that made it possible for foreign subsidiaries of US companies to do some business in Iran. The German and Italian arms of Koch-Glitsch, a Koch subsidiary that makes equipment for oil fields and refineries, won lucrative contracts to supply Iran's Zagros plant, the largest methanol plant in the world. And thanks in part to Koch, methanol is now one of Iran's leading non-oil exports.

So whose side are these guys on? They are on their own side. As estranged brother Bill Koch says about his brothers, their mantra is "Profits above everything else."

According to *Rolling Stone*, in 2008, when oil prices spiked, the Koch brothers realized obscene profits through speculative market betting, after spending $20 million lobbying Congress to stop consumer protection bills: "In comments to the Federal

Trade Commission, Koch lobbyists defended the company's right to rack up fantastic profits at the expense of American consumers. 'A mere attempt to maximize profits cannot constitute market manipulation,' they wrote, adding baldly, 'Excessive profits in the face of shortages are desirable.'"

Again, I reiterate that this is not an indictment of everyone that is super-rich. Neither is it prejudice against people having as much money as they want. For every elitist, condescending plutocrat like Charles and David Koch, there are ten people like Warren Buffet and Bill Gates who are giving their money back to do good in the world and help people in need. Think of the foundations established by Andrew Carnegie, John D. Rockefeller, Henry Ford, and others who have given away billions and billions of dollars for the betterment of the human race. While some of these men were ruthless in their business dealings, many of them eventually came to the conclusion that the only thing to do with their vast fortunes was to give it away.

Not the Koch Brothers, who are also "segregationists" like dad. Fred Koch was a major benefactor, founder, and board member of the John Birch Society (JBS). From the start, JBS was opposed to communism, blaming most of the world's problems on Russia and communism. It is interesting that Fred had no problem making money off of Russia, yet blamed the country for the world's problems. In the 60s, the JBS was opposed to the civil rights movement, calling it a communist plot. Using anti-communist rhetoric, Fred Koch described "integration" as a "Red plot" to "enslave both the white and the black man." JBS claimed that the communists trained Martin Luther King, and that Rosa Parks was a communist. Despite the fact that JBS denounces racism, their actions suggest otherwise.

Charles Koch was also a member of the JBS, according to *The Progressive* and *Center for Media and Democracy*.[21] Charles was an active member during its campaign against the civil rights

movement in the 1960s. In 1968 he resigned his life member-
ship, and ceased his fundraising efforts for the organization, also
ending his advertising in JBS publications. But it is doubtful
that he had a change of heart. What he had instead was an
idea to push his philosophy by hiding behind shell entities (like
Americans for Prosperity) which belied his true intent.

In Wisconsin in 2009, the Koch brothers used their vast
wealth to attack teachers and firefighters and make it harder to
vote; in North Carolina, they promoted segregation. They gave
$22.4 million dollars to think tanks against public education. In
Wake County, North Carolina, Americans for Prosperity—the
Kochs' cover for the new segregation policy called "Neighbor-
hood Schools"—was behind the 2009 election of a majority of
school board members who were against forced busing.[22] The
community was riled up, neighbor fighting neighbor, black
against white, until the next election; then they realized what
had happened to them and threw the Koch brothers' puppets
out of office. This (and other, similar incidents around the
country) show the unbridled arrogance and superiority that the
Koch brothers and their type feel toward the rest of us. They
don't live in Wake County, nor do they have children in school
there. Yet they feel they have the right to dictate to locals how
their children should be educated. They see themselves as gods
who sit up on Olympus, entitled to hurl down their lightning
bolts of money to tell the rest of us how to live. Integration of
the schools after years of racial segregation was one of the most
difficult issues that the people of the South had to face. The
people of Wake County came together and found a way to overcome this contentious issue for the good of their children, white
and black. However, to people like the Koch brothers, it doesn't
matter what the rest of us think—in their minds, their money
makes us inferior subjects, giving them the right to impose their
will upon us. We all need to stand up against these elitists, and

let them know that in America their money does not make them better than the rest of us.

MFA, does their money make them better than the teachers in Newtown, Connecticut, who risked their lives to protect their students from a maniac's gun fire? Does their money make them better than the teachers in Moore, Oklahoma, who threw their bodies over their students to protect them from the deadly tornadoes? Does their money make them better than the nineteen firefighters in Arizona who gave their lives while trying to save others? Bleep NO! To my way of thinking, the Koch brothers aren't good enough to shine these people's shoes. Yet, these individuals and their ilk have the audacity to want to take over our government and dictate how we're supposed to live—all in secret, mind you—because it is beneath them to make their case to us peons by running for public office.

These are dictators trying to control our government. At least Obama was elected by the people. I have a message for the Koch brothers, "One of you get off of your elitist royal butts and run for office." Oh, that's right, they did already. According to the *New York Times*, back in 1980 David Koch ran as a vice presidential candidate on the Libertarian ticket (against George H. W. Bush, who was Reagan's running mate). Koch's "campaign called for the abolition not just of Social Security, federal regulatory agencies and welfare but also of the F.B.I., the C. I. A., and public schools—in other words, any government enterprise that would either inhibit his business profits or increase his taxes."[23] The Libertarian ticket received only one percent of the vote. People saw what he stood for and turned away in droves. So the Koch brothers adopted a new strategy of funneling a hundred million dollars into dozens of propaganda organizations—Freedom Partners, FreedomWorks, Citizens for a Sound Economy, the Cato Institute, Americans for Prosperity—with the goal of buying politicians. In other words, the Kochs seemed to be saying: if the American people won't elect us, we will manipulate them and just buy their government out from under them before they know what happened. Warren Buffet—who, by the way, has more money than they do, has warned us to stop coddling the super-rich! Again, he also said that if there is a class war going on, his class is winning. Edward Bernays, the founder of the modern propaganda industry, described the process as follows:

> Those who manipulate the unseen mechanism of society constitute an invisible government. We are governed, our minds molded, our tastes formed, our ideas suggested largely by men we have never heard of . . . in almost every act of our lives whether in the sphere of politics or business, in our social conduct or our ethical thinking we are dominated by the relatively small number of persons who understand the mental processes and social patterns of the masses. It is they who pull the wires that control the public mind.[24]

Any of our elected officials who are siding with these arrogant monarchists against the rest of us must be voted out of office. I'm not just talking about Congress; the Koch brothers are trying to take over our state and local governments as well. For instance, the Koch brothers and the other "secret kings" have funded an organization called the American Legislative Exchange Council (ALEC) to take over state legislatures. They wine and dine state legislators and then give them "model" pieces of right wing legislation to introduce in their respective state legislatures. An example of the kind of bills they have introduced around the country is the "Stand Your Ground" law, which was highlighted in the Trayvon Martin murder case in Florida.

Regardless of whether you agree with their views or not, we

cannot allow them to buy our elected officials. The almighty vote gives us the true power over our elected officials. If they have sold us out, we need to throw them out. The only question is whether we care enough to look into the record of our elected officials to see if they have been serving us or the would-be kings. There is no substitute for an informed voter.

I understand that most of us have to give every bit of our time and energy just to get by, and have neither the time nor the inclination to pay attention to a political system that seems hopelessly corrupt and unchangeable. But MFA, we have no choice. People like the Koch brothers and some of our largest corporations are using their money and power to buy our government, using it as a tool to further enrich themselves at our expense. If we don't do something about it, they will continue to grind us down to lower and lower standards of living, until the American Dream for most of us is dead. We can blame them for being the arrogant predators that they are. We can blame the traitorous politicians for selling our country out for money and power. However, in the final analysis, the greatest fault lies with us. We are getting exactly what we deserve, because we don't care enough about our country or even ourselves and our families to exercise the amazing power of the vote that we have been blessed with as Americans. Our votes are more powerful than all of the money of these would-be dictators, because we can throw out the flunkies who are doing their bidding. Given what we are up against, we have to shock them and make them fear us. Because we have tolerated their neglect and disrespect for so long, there is no other way to get their attention. We must vote them out. If we do, there will be an astounding and positive change in our government, and our country.

ARE YOU A GREAT AMERICAN?

THE KINDER, GENTLER KOCH BROTHERS' MAKEOVER— THEY CAN'T BE SERIOUS?

YOU MAY HAVE NOTICED THE RECENT FEEL-GOOD TV ADS ABOUT Koch Industries. You may have also noticed that the Koch brothers have suddenly started making "charitable" contributions to organizations and groups that you just wouldn't expect the mean-spirited elitist to give to. For example, there is a new website called "We Are Koch," which touts uplifting stories about Koch employees, and beneficiaries of their philanthropy. Have the would-be kings of America had a change of heart? Don't be ridiculous. The only reason for their attempted image redo is that they have been outed for being exactly what they are—a couple of arrogant, selfish plutocrats, who think they have a right to control our government to use as a tool to make more money for themselves. Their original goal was a stealth takeover of the government. I guess they thought we were too stupid to notice that they were buying every elected official that they could, and getting them to treat the rest of us like dirt. Now they want us all to believe that they are a couple of nice, regular guys who have somehow been misunderstood.

If so, then why has this makeover campaign only started

after the brothers' meanness and greed was exposed? There has been a great deal of controversy by some who say that organizations shouldn't take money from people as dastardly as the Koch brothers. I disagree. There is an old saying in politics: "Sometimes the jackasses are on your side." If the money allows these organizations to do some good, and there are no strings attached, then they should take it. However, let us be perfectly clear about the main reason that the Koch brothers and their ilk are throwing all of this money around. It is not about politics or charity. As their own brother said, above all, these guys are about profit. These are investments, and they expect a huge return. Over the years, they have spent hundreds of millions of dollars to gradually take over our government. The brothers recently stated that they intend to spend nearly $900 million for political campaigns in 2016. What that really means is that they are willing to spend a billion to buy mainly Republican politicians to do their bidding. Let's face it; they practically own the Republican Party already, through the Tea Party. Now, all they need to complete their takeover is to own the President of the United States. Most of the 2016 Republican presidential candidates are already in line, begging them for money.

So when it comes to knowing what the Koch brothers are really about, remember what Maya Angelou said, "When someone shows you who they are, believe them the first time."[25]

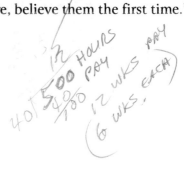

> IF FOR NO OTHER REASON, WE OWE IT TO THOSE WHO GAVE THEIR "LAST FULL MEASURE OF DEVOTION" TO EXERCISE THE RIGHTS THAT THEY SACRIFICED EVERYTHING FOR

	Killed	Wounded
1. Revoulutionary War	25,000	25,000
2. War of 1812	15,000	4,505
3. Civil War	364,511(Union) 299,524(Confederate)	281,881 Unsure
4. Mexican-American War	11,550	13,283
5. Phillipine-American War	4,196	2,930
6. World War I	116,516	204,002
7. World War II	405,399	670,846
8. Korean War	36,516	92,134
9. Vietnam War	58,209	153,303
10. Gulf War	294	849
11. War on Terror		
Iraq	4,488	32,222
Afghanistan	2,229	18,675
Total for all Conflicts	**1,321,612**	**1,531,036**

THROUGHOUT THIS BOOK, I HAVE ASKED IF WE ARE "GREAT AMERI-cans" to urge us to think and to care enough to use the great power of our vote for the betterment of our country and ourselves. We seem to live in a time when we refuse to tolerate inconvenience, let alone be willing to make real sacrifices. However, as you can see from the above, so many Americans have made the ultimate sacrifice for our democracy and for our right to vote.

As I said earlier, I did not serve in the military. Nevertheless, as an immediate post-World War II baby boomer, I could not help but have the deepest appreciation and respect for those in the "greatest generation" who gave all for our freedom.

As a kid, I saw every war movie that came out, read all of the war comic books, and played army with toy military weapons. I graduated from a military high school. However, none of this even hinted at how terrible war really is. As time has passed, movies and documentaries about war have become more and more honest and realistic, frequently portraying the utter horror that our soldiers faced with unimaginable courage and determination. They are difficult to watch—but even so, the reality was worse. It is impossible to imagine what it was like to be there. Yet in the midst of hell on earth, our military has gotten the job done every time. That includes the Vietnam War—my generation's war. Even though our involvement there was a tragic mistake, our armed forces fought just as hard and just as bravely as our soldiers did in any other war, and accomplished every military objective that they were ordered to undertake. The blame and the disrespect that was heaped upon those who fought in Vietnam is one of the greatest injustices of our time. They didn't get us into that war. Our leaders did. Instead of showing them gratitude for their sacrifice, we scorned and reviled them. May we never demean the sacrifices of our military that way again. The duty of the combat soldier was perhaps best described many years ago by Alfred, Lord Tennyson, when he wrote—in the poem, "The Charge of the Light Brigade"—"Theirs not to reason why / Theirs but to do and die."[26]

THE WAR OF WARS—OUR VERY OWN WAR

There are many reasons the Civil War stands out from the rest. More American soldiers were killed in it than in any other war. The fighting was some of the most vicious and courageous in the history of warfare. However, what obviously distinguishes it the most is that we were fighting and killing each other. Somehow, all of the terrible things about war are magnified even more when fellow countrymen turn on each other. 750,000 soldiers died in that war. That was two percent of the population at the time. Today, that would be the equivalent of six million dead. Think of the American ancestry that was lost with these men.

Today, we cannot comprehend the depths of the division and animosity that existed in our country at the end of the Civil War. Words such as hatred and loathing are insufficient to describe it. Black people understand it best because white southerners took it all out on us. Yet, despite it all, we pulled together to become this great nation that has repeatedly shown that we can accomplish anything when we stand together as a people. President Lincoln said it best: a house divided against itself cannot stand. United we stand, divided we fall. Unfortunately, there are people in our own country whose main goal in life is to divide us. They do it out of selfishness, greed, and arrogance. They could not care less if they hurt the country and its people—as long as they get more money and power to satisfy their sick, overinflated egos. In their minds, they are bigger and more important than the country. The rest of us are just the "great unwashed"—a term used to describe the working class, who came from the fields and mines—to be exploited for their benefit. They trample on the spirit and principles of freedom, fairness, and opportunity that this country was founded upon. They are as un-American as can be.

Again, the simple fact is that none of us are going anywhere and there is plenty of opportunity for all of us. The different backgrounds of Americans, this melting pot, have brought nothing but strength and richness to our country. If we could come together after the bitterness of the Civil War, surely we can overcome any differences of opinion that we have today on any subject in order to join together and make our country better for all of us and the world.

If our armed forces had not sacrificed their bodies, minds, and lives over the years, there would be no United States of America. If for no other reason than to honor them, mustn't we join together—as they did—to make our country the best that it can be? Can't we at least care enough to vote? We must elect leaders who want to bring us together, instead of tearing the country apart.

ARE YOU A GREAT AMERICAN?

WE THE PEOPLE . . . ARE THE GREATEST POLITICAL POWER ON EARTH!

THE AMERICAN PEOPLE ARE THE GREATEST POLITICAL POWER ON earth, because we can control the destiny and the wellbeing of its most powerful nation. Each of us is endowed with a piece of that power. All we have to do is care enough to exercise it for the better. I am grateful for the people all over the country who protested against the killing of Michael Brown, an unarmed black teen in Ferguson, Missouri; and the killing of Eric Garner, an unarmed black man standing on the street in New York and many similar cases that are coming to light recently. Garner had just broken up a fight, and was surrounded by white police officers, who put him in a chokehold after he asked them to leave him alone. He died as he cried out, "I can't breathe." However, as much as protesting is a constitutional right, we must also channel our energy to voting the people out of office who use their authority to abuse us.

We have the power to make our elected officials snap to attention and salute us, instead of just kissing the rear ends of the rich and powerful. We just need to tell them what we want, and really mean it. Given the utter lack of respect that they show us now, the only way to convince them that we mean it is to vote them out of office. Anything short of that will be looked upon as a sign that we are still a bunch of suckers who will never hold them accountable, regardless of how much they harm us.

So how do we know whether to vote them out or not? We make fair and reasonable demands that are good for the country and all of We the People. Before Election Day, ask them where they stand on issues that are important to you, or the issues I've mentioned in this book's last chapter: "Handbook for Being a Great American." Ask them specifically if they will support (and most importantly, vote) for your issues. If they say no, let them know with certainty that you will vote for their opponent. If their opponent also says no, start a write-in campaign for someone (yourself?) who will represent all the people. While it is true that write-in campaigns seldom succeed, it is not impossible for them to do so. In Alaska, a United States Senator was elected by a write-in campaign when the people were dissatisfied with the candidate chosen by their party. These days, anything is possible through the use of social media. If the candidate who won lies to you, you must hold them accountable: vote them out the next time.

Most importantly, follow the money to its source. Remember, you can tell a lot about your candidate by paying attention to where they get their money from. Due to the Supreme Court's ruling creating Super PACs, it is often difficult to find out who is behind the campaign ads and politicians. They are not required to report their financial sources. But regardless of what the Supreme Court says, we have an absolute right to know where that money came from. Ask the candidates themselves. If they won't tell you, don't vote for them, you have your answer.

There are also unbiased organizations—such as Vote Smart and the League of Women Voters—which provide a wealth of information on the candidates and issues on a particular ballot.

With a click of the mouse, you can find out the kind of people, organizations, and causes that are supporting a candidate. If they are running for re-election, you can find out how they really voted on issues of importance to you.

Then there is "The Great American Cop-Out"—low voter turnout! That is what most politicians want us to do. We play right into their hands when we stay home or shrug our shoulders as if it doesn't matter. The truth is that our votes have the power to change everything! Are you a Great American?

DEAR MR. PRESIDENT

You inherited from your predecessor one of the biggest messes that an incoming President has ever had to face: two wars, an economy on the brink of collapse, and a monstrous budget deficit. Since your inauguration, you have been under incessant, vicious, racially motivated attacks from the Republican Tea Party, their super-rich owners, and the ultra–right-wing propagandists at Fox News. Despite this, you have conducted yourself as a true gentleman and statesman, with a dignity that befits the highest office. You have dealt with one overwhelming issue after another, with reassuring, genuine competency.

When you reached out to the Republican Tea Party in a spirit of cooperation and they completely rebuffed you every time, I wanted to tell you that they were never going to cooperate with you anymore than they would've let me sit in the front of the bus when I was growing up in Georgia. They weren't rejecting your overtures because of your politics. They were rejecting you because you were black. You can't say that, because you would be accused of "playing the race card" (whatever that means). I grew up under racism. I know it when I see it. Some of the Republicans, especially those who are also in the Tea Party, are just straight, cold racists. The Koch brothers founded and funded Americans for Prosperity, which is for re-segregation, and which provided education and funding for the Tea Party, appealing to people's racism to attack you. What I don't understand is why you have wasted so much time and energy in the pointless exercise of seeking their cooperation, when it was clear that they were all take and absolutely no give—and that it was going to be that way for as long as you were in office. In my opinion, you ended up making serious concessions on important issues, for which you got nothing in return. I know that politics is the art of compromise. However, that adage is meaningless if the other side has no intention whatever of cooperating.

Mr. President, even in the face of the relentless attacks of these hate-mongers, you have achieved a string of historic accomplishments, particularly concerning issues of fairness and equality. Your appointments to the Supreme Court have been superb. You have deftly navigated us through some of the most difficult foreign policy challenges that our country has ever faced. When the opportunity presented itself, you ordered the execution of the man responsible for murdering thousands of Americans on September 11. The Affordable Care Act will go down in history as one of the most significant accomplishments of any administration. Ironically, the fact that your enemies named it "ObamaCare" will ensure that it is one of the greatest tributes to you and your legacy.

Nevertheless, Mr. President, some of your actions have been truly troubling and disappointing. The first is the appointment of Jack Lew as Secretary of the Treasury. Citi Group, his former employer, was one of the banks most responsible for the 2008 financial crisis. His predecessors, who set the policies that led us to the meltdown, were also Wall Street bankers. After all of the damage that these bankers did to the economy and so many people's lives, how could you put yet another one of these people in charge of the country's finances? Obviously I don't know Mr. Lew personally, but his predecessors have shown that their first loyalty is to their profession and their banks, not the country's finances. Worst of all, these bankers are fighting your every attempt to

I WANTED LABOR LAWS THAT WOULD ALLOW WORKERS TO JOIN IN THE FIGHT FOR BETTER HEALTHY & SOCIALLY POSITIVE WORK CONDITIONS, & NOT JUST INCOME & BENEFITS. I GUESS THAT PUTS ME INTO THE CONSTITUTIONAL PERFECTIONIST CAMP.

Handwritten at top: NO, POLITICS IS ALL ABOUT HALF BAKED DECISIONS THAT FAVOR A FEW & USUALLY DELUDE VOTERS w/ GOOD INTENTIONS WHILE HIDING BAD FACTS,

reform them so they don't destroy the economy again. You are too close to these people.

With respect to ObamaCare, you had deep support from the people to include the Public Option. It appears that if you had truly pressed the issue, it would have been included and made it a much better bill and easier to implement.

In the Farm Bill, you gave big agri-businesses all the subsidies that they wanted while agreeing to cuts to programs for the neediest Americans. Mr. President, forty-six million Americans live below the poverty line. One in five children lives in poverty. We know that the hateful Republican Tea Party wants to punish everybody but the super-rich. How could you compromise with them on the backs of the people that are truly hurting? How could you not fight for the underprivileged in this case?

With regard to immigration reform, we know that the Republican Tea Party will never cooperate with you. They only want things to get worse so they can continue to scapegoat farm workers for political gain. However, there are reforms that you can implement as president. One of the first tasks should be to stop the rape and sexual abuse of women farm workers in the fields. Federal government agencies know about this and are doing nothing. Why are you hesitating to implement them? How many times during our civil rights movement did the powerful keep telling us to "be patient" or that "the time is not right"? There was always some excuse for not taking action. But politically speaking, there is never a "right time" to fight serious injustice. It is never easy. As we used to say back to the critics, "If not now, then when?!"

You must be saying, who the hell are you to criticize me without having any idea of the enormous opposition and the incredibly difficult decisions I face? That is more than a fair question. However, Mr. President, I assure you that I understand why you suddenly have more gray hair than I do—even though I am your elder by 14 years. My political career consists of serving in my state's legislature, holding a statewide office, and unsuccessfully running for governor (twice). In contrast, you broke through the most difficult color barrier in the history of our country

Handwritten right margin: i.e. ALL LAWS GET CORRUPTED IN ADMINISTRATION & FOLLOW-UP HAS TO BE GENEROUS IF TRUE LAWS ARE TO BE CONTINUED.

on your first try—and then you were reelected! Every African American who has overcome any significant racial barrier has had to be an exceptional human being. In order to become the first African American president of the United States, you just about had to have an "S" on your chest. You did it. You achieved what many thought impossible. You connected with the American people in a way that few Presidential candidates ever have, and most of us have stuck by you.

What is disappointing and puzzling is that you have not turned to us to help you overcome the intransigent, bigoted bomb-throwers of the ultra-right wing Republican Tea Party and the super-rich who fund them. You seem to have become a Washington D.C. insider, trying to play a game that they want to stop you from winning at any cost, including hurting the country and the people. The inside of that Beltway has become a cesspool of special interest money that has totally corrupted our government. The only thing that is more powerful than all of that money is We the People, because we can vote corrupt politicians out of office.

You have less than a year left in office. Get out of that hellhole that our nation's capital has become and take your case to us. You have nothing to lose. The concept of being a "lame duck" is a myth. Let us help you make our country better. Most importantly, many if not most Americans feel powerless to affect our government. We need our President to remind us that our government belongs to us and really is "of the People, by the People and for the People" by asking us to exercise the inherent power guaranteed to us by the Constitution.

Sincerely,
One of We the People

THE REAL ENEMY IS US!

As unjust and unethical as it is that elected officials and even the United States Supreme Court would conspire to take away our right to vote, they are not the main problem. Once again, the real problem is us. This country has given us this great power of true democracy with our votes and we could care less. According to the *New York Times*, more than 50 million Americans are not registered to vote.[27] Our voter turnout for the 2014 election was 36.3 percent of eligible voters. That was the lowest since World War II. The voter turnout for African Americans was 35 percent. My brothers and sisters, if there is anyone who should understand the great might of the vote it is "We the Black People." Our ancestors were beaten, chewed on by police dogs, and murdered so we could be full-fledged Americans by casting our votes.

I'm not just talking about our beloved heroes Dr. King and Malcolm X. There are so many that we will never know of who sacrificed so much so we could transform the country with our votes and help elect the first African American president. The great, hard lesson that we should have learned for all time is that we can't afford not to vote. Today, we have a new generation of racists and elitists who want to take away our hard-earned right to vote. We have paid too high a price to throw the power of our votes away by not using them. For our own sake today, and out of respect for our heroes of the past, we should always have the highest voter turnout in every election.

Our brothers and sisters in Mississippi clearly understand this. We must follow their lead. In the 2014 election, when a radical right wing Tea Party candidate was campaigning on rolling back to the "old days" in terms of civil rights, the black voters of Mississippi used their votes to defeat him. Not only did they defeat him, they did it by beating the radical right-wingers at their own game. One of the radical right's tactics has been to push state legislatures to pass laws for "Open Primary" elections, which allow the members of a party to vote in the other party's primary election. Their strategy is to get their voters to vote against and defeat the strongest candidate in the other party. The Mississippi legislature passed such a law.

Even though most African Americans in Mississippi are Democrats, during the primary they used the law to cross over and defeat the Tea Party candidate by voting for his opponent. They accomplished this because they were vigilant and organized. They understood what a huge difference their votes could make. They remembered that no state fought harder to deny us the right to vote than Mississippi. They also remembered the courage and sacrifice shown by those who won that fight so that subsequent victories would be possible.

To understand the great power of the vote and how to use it we also need to look at the Lesbian, Gay, Bisexual, and Transgender (LGBT) community. There are few groups in recent times who have been subjected to such near-universal and accepted bigotry.

Being part of this group was considered one of the worst stigmas in our society. Many assumed it was okay to harass and beat gay people. Discrimination came even from those who belonged to minority groups that experienced prejudice themselves. What is particularly difficult about the intolerance toward gay people is that members of their own families often carry it out. I don't know what I would have done if my mother had not protected and encouraged me in the face of racial segregation.

Not that long ago, many gay Americans were forced to hide their sexual identity. If they admitted that they were gay (or were "outed"), they faced social and economic ruin. Blackmail was a constant threat. J. Edgar Hoover (the long-time head of the FBI), for instance, systematically blackmailed gay Americans to get information that he sought.

Compare that to today. The United States Supreme Court just handed down an opinion which says that gay marriage is the law of the land. To say that this is a landmark decision is a gross understatement. I'm old enough to remember a time when the idea of gay marriage would not have occurred to even those with the wildest of imaginations. Compare that to what happened when Tim Cook, the CEO of Apple, Inc. (America's largest corporation), publicly announced that he was gay. Public reaction was minimal at best. However, for someone my age, this was an amazing occurrence. I can remember when it would have been beyond comprehension. There are a number of reasons for this amazing change in attitude toward individuals in the LGBT community. The main reason, of course, is that this is America. Despite all of the injustices that some Americans have suffered and still suffer, the American people, sometimes much too slowly, truly want to live by the principles in our Constitution—principles of freedom, fairness, and opportunity for all.

Nevertheless, those of us who have been discriminated against have had to stand up and absolutely demand our full rights as

Americans. Even then, we also have to know that we will not be treated fully as Americans until we actually exercise our rights. The most important of these rights is the right to vote. The incredible victory for the LGBT community happened because they established themselves as one of the most powerful political forces in the nation—by being politically active, contributing money to candidates, and, most importantly, demonstrating that they vote.

The great question before our country now is when will middle-class Americans, especially the white middle class, finally wake up and realize that now they are the new "n" words and are being discriminated against and exploited. If you are white, maybe you can't see this because this kind of treatment used to be reserved for us (African Americans). But the fact is that they are treating you with disdain and you are getting poorer and poorer. They are taking the American Dream away from you and your children by refusing to invest in the education and training that leads to opportunities for higher-paying jobs, occupations, and professions. Our elected officials have sold you out to some of the super-rich elitists, seeing you as cheap labor, just like they saw us.

When are you going to rise up—like us "n words" and other "minorities" had to do—and vote these people out of office? When are you going to learn what we had to learn the hard way? To politicians, if you don't vote, you are a nobody. If you don't care enough to vote, you give all of your power to those who do. The reason that groups like the NRA and the LGBT community have so much influence over politicians is because they vote. The reason the middle class is being abused is because politicians know that we won't hold them accountable with our votes. Take back your power. Be a Great American. VOTE!

CHECK THE FACTS

Currently, Congress' approval rating is in the single digits, and has been for years. So why do we keep sending the same people back again and again? The reason is that most of us have no idea what our elected officials really stand for. Frankly, we tend to vote for the candidate that spends the most money. That is why the would-be kings and queens now own our government. They know that all they have to do to manipulate us is drown us with two-minute sound bites. They know that we are not going to look at their voting records, at whom they get their money from, or at their attendance records. There is also the tendency to think that my Representative or Senator is not as bad as the rest of them. That may be true, but you really don't know until you check. Let me state the obvious. Politicians are not always what they seem to be. So, check your Congress members' voting records, attendance records, and whom they get their campaign money from. Of course, the same applies to state and local elected officials. Also, remember that members of Congress have offices in their home states and districts, should you wish to contact them directly.

There are two groups that provide unbiased and balanced information regarding candidates and ballot measures.

Project Vote Smart (votesmart.org) is run by volunteers, and takes no money from special interest groups. No one can join Vote Smart's board without a political opposite. People as diverse as former Presidents Carter and Ford, former Senators McGovern and Goldwater, former Governor Dukakis, former Congresswoman Ferraro, and current US Senator McCain have served on Vote Smart's board, ensuring balance and strict impartiality in Vote Smart programs and services. You can find out how much money the candidates received and from whom, and review voting records and public statements made by the candidates as well as their positions on the issues. Vote Smart also enables you to see how different interest groups rated your candidate, if they are running for re-election.

The League of Women Voters, a non-partisan civic organization, is rooted in the movement that secured the right to vote for women. Founded in 1920, the League has worked to foster civic engagement, provide education, and enhance access to the vote across America in local, state, and federal elections. They take no position for or against a candidate, focusing rather on education. The League provides personalized online voter guides for easy use. Check out Vote411.org—put in your address and you will receive information about candidates and issues in your area.

IMPORTANT ISSUES

Here is a list of issues that I consider to be non-partisan and of great concern to our country as a whole. They are primarily aimed at the members of Congress and the President. However, the same process of accountability applies to state and local levels of government as well.

EDUCATION

1. **Allocate funds to rehire the thousands of teachers, kindergarten through high school, who we laid off as a result of the 2008 financial crisis.**

   If we really care anything about our children and the future of our country, our young people must receive the best education, so they and our country can compete in the global economy. Currently, we are falling further and further behind.

   Most importantly, education is the great equalizer that gives every young person a chance to achieve the American Dream, regardless of background. This is the essence of what America is all about.

2. **Give students and parents serious relief from student loan debt.**

   Our nation's staggering one trillion dollars in student

loan debt is not the fault of the students or parents who co-signed for these loans. It is the fault of the bloated, greedy Wall Street bankers who killed the jobs that these students would have gotten upon graduation. Our alleged leaders in Washington bailed these incompetent porkers out with hundreds of billions of our tax dollars in no interest loans to save them from bankruptcy. If they won't help us victims of these robber barons, they must be voted out of office.

LIBERTARIANS!

3. **Invest in a "GI Bill" for education and training for all Americans.**

THEY DON'T SEE THAT ITS THEIR JOB TO CREATE JOBS,

Again, our country would not be the wealthiest in the world if we had not invested in our soldiers' education and training after they returned from World War II. If the arrogant jerks currently in Washington really cared about improving the economy and creating jobs, they would invest in us also. Yet you don't even hear the words "education and training" come out of Washington these days. That is because our politicians, especially the Republicans, do not want us to get an education. They only want us for cheap labor—just like it was for black people in the south. They want as many of us stuck in minimum wage jobs as possible. When is the middle class, especially the white middle class, going to realize that now we are all the new "n" words? If we don't wake up and get some fight in us, we are all going to end up living the modern-day equivalent of picking cotton.

I WONDER IF THEY OPPOSE TAX CREDITS FOR BUSINESS LOSSES, OR R + D EXPENSES?

The stronger, the healthier and the wealthier the middle class is, the stronger, healthier and wealthier our country will be.

Remember back to the 1990s, when the main campaign slogan was "It's the economy, stupid"? Our battle cry must be, "WE ARE THE ECONOMY, STUPID!"

If an incumbent or candidate refuses to invest in our

talent and skills so we can better our country, and ourselves, they are too stupid to hold public office. Toss them out, or don't vote for them.

ECONOMY

1. **Break up these banks that have been designated as "too big to fail." Reinstate the Glass-Steagall law.**

What "too big to fail" really means is that us taxpayers will again have to bail these bloated banks out every time they take down the economy due to their limitless greed and incompetence.

Failure is just as important to free enterprise as success. Competition is the foundation of free enterprise. Businesses fail every day. Nobody bails them out. If these banks are too big to fail, they are simply too big according to any genuine concept of free enterprise.

MFA, these banks cost us 8.7 million jobs. It has taken us six years to recover that number of jobs, but many of the ones we have replaced them with pay less than the ones lost. Think of where we, and our country, would be if 8.7 million jobs had been *added* on top of the 8.7 million we already had. This recession was caused purely by the banks. Indeed, they almost caused the entire global economy to collapse. Worse, they got away with it, because they, along with other rich and powerful interests, own our government.

The paltry fines that have been assessed against these behemoths don't even amount to a "slap on the wrist." They will recoup the amount of these fines in several days of earnings. The top management of these banks was not personally fined at all. Remember, after we bailed them out with hundreds of billions of our tax dollars, after they cost us millions of jobs, foreclosures, and bankruptcies, they gave themselves the largest salaries and bonuses in their history. That is not merely spitting in our faces. That is kicking us to the ground and urinating on us, and with the help of our so-called leaders. Worst of all, we're just laying here and taking it, by re-electing the same people over and over again. We must demand that criminal charges be filed against these banks—and in particular against the top management, who were personally responsible for the misconduct.

The Glass-Steagall Law had protected us from the greed and recklessness of these bankers since the Great Depression, by keeping our deposits safe from the banks' investment functions. Banks could not use our deposits to make risky investments. But then big banks spent hundreds of millions of dollars lobbying and making political contributions to Republicans and Democrats, in the hope of repealing this necessary legislation. Once they succeeded, they proceeded to invest our deposits in mortgages that were all but worthless. This is how they caused the financial crisis. Their arrogance and greed will cause them to do it again and again if we let them. Glass-Steagall must be re-enacted before they cause another crisis. DONE — THEN UNDONE BY TRUMP!

2. **Enact tax reform.**

Two-thirds of corporations in our country pay no federal income taxes at all, while the rest of us suckers have our taxes withheld from every paycheck. That's right—your son or daughter with only a summer job paid more taxes than CitiGroup did between 2008 and 2012. CitiGroup paid no federal income tax for four years. Among the Wall Street banks that caused the financial collapse of 2008, CitiGroup was one of the worst offenders. Yet we bailed them out of bankruptcy with $476 billion of our tax dollars, which they then used not only to make themselves profitable, but to give themselves huge bonuses. On top of all that, they pay no taxes. What a deal! And CitiGroup was not alone. Twenty-six of our largest corporations paid no federal income taxes between 2008 and 2012.

How could this be? Well, ask your Congressperson. He or she—whether a Democrat or a Republican—probably voted to give the banks enough loopholes to dodge all taxes. When asked about why they pay little or no taxes, the banks' response is always that they are only doing what the law allows. The problem is that they are in effect *writing* the laws, spending huge amounts of money on lobbyists and campaign contributions to get them passed.

Why is this a problem for the rest of us? When banks don't pay their fair share of taxes, the tax burden is shifted to the rest of us chumps, who have no choice but to pay. The government certainly doesn't spend less. The rest of us patsies get to make up for what the rich and powerful refuse to pay. Of course, nobody *wants* to pay taxes. But some of us have no choice. The real difference between the banks and us is that they pay no taxes and get richer. If we refuse to pay our taxes, the government takes everything we own and sends us to prison.

Our Senators and Representatives know that we are being hosed, but they don't care, because the rest of us are not rich and powerful enough to hire lobbyists, or give large amounts of campaign cash. MFA, what our elected officials have long forgotten is that we elected them to "lobby" for us. They have totally abdicated that responsibility in order to ingratiate themselves to those with money and power. They know that the middle class is slowly being ground into poverty. They yammer on and on about creating jobs, when they know for a fact that these giant corporations are avoiding paying taxes by keeping their profits "offshore" (i.e., in other countries). In other words, these giant "American" corporations are paying no taxes and then using the money they save to create jobs in other countries—jobs that could and should be here at home. Some of these corporations have even moved their headquarters to other countries, to avoid paying taxes to the country that built them, and the country that buys most of their products. "God Bless America, My Home Sweet Home," indeed. I wonder which flag they pledge allegiance to.

Again, if tax reform is to happen, our Senators and Representatives have to know that we are deadly serious about voting them out of office if they don't get it done. Right now, they assume that we will not hold them accountable because we haven't done so in the past. Ask your incumbent or candidate if they will work to create a tax system that is fair for all of us. If they refuse to do so, or if they lie, throw them out or don't vote for them. They are in somebody's pocket, and they don't care about the majority of us.

CAMPAIGN FINANCE REFORM

It is not an exaggeration to say that our nation's capital and our elected officials have become so preoccupied with raising money that they have sold our government out to the highest bidders, and most of the American people along with it. In a 2015 interview with *USA Today*'s Capital Download, the new Senate Majority leader, Republican Mitch McConnell, was "defiant on the right of the Koch brothers' political network to spend close to a billion dollars before the 2016 elections, clearly delighted with his new status as majority leader."[28] McConnell is actually proud of selling himself, and selling us out.

At the risk of being overly graphic, when it comes to money, what Washington, D.C. needs is one giant enema, in the form of campaign finance reform. It has been said that money is the mother's milk of politics. I'm afraid that we have gone well beyond that. Money is now the heroin of politics. Like drug dealers, people such as the Koch brothers and their ilk are more than willing to supply our addicted elected officials with all the "drug money" they want, as long as they are willing to sell their souls and do exactly as they are told. Does your Representative or Senator represent you and your fellow constituents, or have they sold you, and our country, to the super-rich and powerful? If they have refused to support and vote for campaign finance reform, you have your answer. Don't vote for them.

WARNING: After we "administer" campaign finance reform to them, head for the highest ground you can find and get a gas mask.

We need to get the money out of politics, so that politicians are beholden to us instead of the super-rich. James Madison, the fourth president of the US, was an advocate of the First Amendment. His desire was for political equality in the face of economic inequality. And yet we have swung so far from that ideal, given that two people (the Koch brothers) can dump in a billion dollars to try to control our political system.

Recently, a new Super PAC known as Mayday PAC began fighting back, with a grass-roots campaign funded by thousands of small donors, and a few high rollers too. Instead of pushing for restrictions on giving, Mayday PAC has been looking for ways to spur more giving by small donors, in order to counteract big donors' control of elections. The idea is to fight money with money. Mayday PAC was created by Lawrence Lessig, a professor at Harvard Law School who has ties to Silicon Valley, and Mark McKinnon, a former adviser to President George W. Bush. The idea is to attract both liberals and conservatives who want to dilute the influence of big donors in elections. As reported by MayDay.us

> Our framers gave us a "representative democracy"-what they called, "a Republic." But that Republic was to be

representative of all of us. Congress, as Madison said, was to be "dependent on the People alone." And by "the People," as he explained in Federalist 52, he meant "not the rich, more than the poor."

We have allowed Congress to betray this fundamental commitment. We don't have a representative branch "dependent on the People alone." Instead, we have a Congress "dependent on their funders."

That dependency produces a government obsessed with the interests of the rich more than the poor.[29]

One of Mayday's initiatives is to ask voters to ask members of Congress to become #Leaders4Reform, by cosponsoring legislation that will reverse the corrupting influence of money in our elections. As reported by Fair Politics, Mayday.us says, "Congress depends on a tiny number of funders to run their campaigns. Each of the following five proposals would decentralize the funding of elections, either through matching funds or democracy vouchers, so that Congress is dependent on all citizens."[30] The proposals are sponsored by both Republicans and Democrats and include the "Government by the People Act," the "Political Money Reform Proposal," the "Empowering Citizens Act," and the "Taxation Only with Representation Act."[31]

Many of our states and localities have tried different forms of public finance or restrictions on contributions. Some have worked, and some have been struck down by the courts, but we must keep trying. We must put our best minds on the task of dealing with the economic inequalities of running for office, and counteracting the plutocrats who threaten government by and for the people. Check out "mayday.us" and decide for yourself if this is the route to go. Whatever happens, we must not give up. As *Forbes* recently wrote:

> The mortal struggle at hand today is not between the right and the left. It is not between the Congress and

NO, IT'S THE OUTSIDERS BUYING THE INSIDERS

president. It is between us voters (currently outsiders to our own government) and the Washington Insiders.[32]

IMMIGRATION REFORM

Give me your tired, your poor,
Your huddled masses yearning to breathe free,
The wretched refuse of your teeming shore.
Send these, the homeless, tempest-tossed, to me:
I lift my lamp beside the golden door.[33]

(Written in 1883 by American poet Emma
Lazarus, and inscribed on the Statue of Liberty.)

Before I moved to Oregon in 1974, I had not lived in an area where there was a large Latino population. The depth of the prejudice against Latinos shocked me. Their long, bitter struggle for equality obviously continues. We all recognize that the states along the US–Mexico border are flashpoints for undocumented workers trying to enter the United States. But that doesn't justify the blatant disrespect we're seeing in this day and age. When the Arizona Legislature, for instance, passed a law requiring Americans who happen to be of Hispanic descent to produce documentation to prove their citizenship, they were blatantly declaring that they could treat a United States citizen unequally, solely on the basis of his or her ethnic background. This is reminiscent of when we imprisoned Japanese American citizens in camps during World War II because of their Japanese heritage—even though the US Supreme Court declared such laws unconstitutional years ago.

Our enforcement of immigration laws is total hypocrisy. We rant against people crossing our borders illegally. Then we turn around and hire them to do the kind of work that we refuse to do for ourselves. Their cheap labor keeps our food prices low, and yet some of us want to deport them all. We know for a fact that if we did so, our economy and our day-to-day lives would be totally disrupted.

Instead of beginning to solve this problem—by recognizing that we absolutely need immigrant labor and that immigrants need the jobs to get out of staggering poverty—our Congress lets the situation fester and become more divisive. The Republican Tea Party refuses to even discuss the issue. They would rather appeal to people's fear and bigotry—sentiments they obviously agree with. This could and should be a win-win situation for our economy and their economic needs if these demagogues would cooperate. Throw these obstructionists out of office.

Then there are those large corporations who see immigration as a way to bring needed talent into our country. The question is why should we have to go outside of the country to get talent? We have some of the best colleges and universities in the world. We just need to give our own people a better opportunity to attend them.

ELECTION LAW REFORM

Contrary to the Citizen United decision handed down by the five pseudo-Justices on the US Supreme Court—Scalia, Roberts, Thomas, Alito, and Kennedy—we have an absolute right to know where the people we elect get their campaign money from. We must force our elected officials, especially in Congress, to pass laws to bring complete transparency to campaign contributions and expenditures. We must insist on limits for all campaign contributions, and ensure that all of them are reported.

One institution after another is letting us down, and the US Supreme court is no exception. We have a right to know who is trying to buy our government out from under us. Demand transparency. You are entitled to know!

BACKGROUND CHECKS

How many innocent people have to die before we stop cowering before the radical, uncompromising few when it comes to gun violence?

I am a gun owner. I owned my first .22 rifle before I was ten years old. At one time when I was a teenager, I owned four guns. I graduated from a Catholic military school: St. Emma Military Academy in Virginia. I was on my company's rifle team. Each cadet was issued an M1 Garand. Also in our armory were six M1 Carbines, six .45 caliber 1911 pistols, four Browning Automatic Rifles (BARs), a 106 mm. recoilless rifle with a .50 spotting rifle on top, and an 81 mm mortar. Once a year we were inspected by the United States Army, at which time we had to show proficiency by firing every type of weapon in our armory (except for the 106 mm recoilless, because it was too powerful to fire for the school's location—although we did fire the .50 caliber spotting rifle on top). I had the incredible honor and experience, during one of our federal inspections, of firing the 81 mm mortar. So unless you are or were in the military, very few gun owners in America have anything on me when it comes to firing weapons.

I do not believe that guns are somehow inherently evil. I don't hunt anymore, but I have no problem with legal hunting. As with our other freedoms, I do not believe that restrictions should be placed on gun ownership unless it is truly necessary. As a candidate and elected official, I was consistently endorsed by the Oregon chapter of the National Rifle Association (NRA). I respect that gun ownership is an important part of American culture. I believe that unreasonable restrictions on gun ownership would be counterproductive, causing the same detrimental results as Prohibition did—making criminals out of otherwise law-abiding people, and embedding the scourge of organized crime in our society.

However, even though we repealed Prohibition, we still have reasonable restrictions on the use and sale of alcohol. With respect to gun ownership, it is not unreasonable to run a background check on a person before you sell them a gun. It is no more unreasonable to refuse to sell a gun to someone who has a criminal background than it is to refuse to allow someone to drive who has had their driver's license taken away because of repeated drunk driving offenses. Most Americans agree. According to a 2013 poll, nearly seventy-four percent of NRA members support universal background checks. Obviously, the vast majority of those who wish to buy a gun would pass a background check. So why did a bill establishing background checks fail in Congress?

The reason is that key members of Congress, along with the leadership of the National NRA, are too cowardly to stand up to those with views on gun ownership that are so extreme as to border on the ridiculous and the obsessive. If we were talking about owning a driver's license instead of gun ownership, these people would be insisting that even serial drunk drivers have a right to drive a car. Out of selfishness and paranoia, these extremists refuse to acknowledge that those who abuse their freedoms and rights lose their freedoms and rights. When you drive drunk, you lose your right to drive. When you become a criminal, you lose your right to own a gun.

Background checks are not a cure-all for gun violence. However, they are a simple and effective way of keeping some guns out of the hands of some who should not have them. The point is that background checks work, and that most Americans and law enforcement officers want them. If we voted, elected officials would listen to us instead of the extremists. We must demand that our lawmakers take this small step of implementing background checks to keep guns out of the hands of criminals and to make a strong statement against the tragic, senseless gun violence that is taking the lives of so many innocent people.

Are you a Great American?

STOP THE WAR ON WOMEN

Use of the word "war" is not an exaggeration. One in three women have been raped in our military. One in five women are being raped on our college campuses. Recently, 70,000 unprocessed rape kits were found in a few police agencies that were actually investigated across the country, leading *USA Today* to estimate that the number of untested rape kits actually reaches into the hundreds of thousands.[34] These rape kits preserve the evidence of rape: when a victim reports a sexual assault, a medical professional conducts a thorough examination of the victim's entire body, in an attempt to find any DNA evidence left behind by the attacker. This is an extremely powerful tool for solving a crime or exonerating the falsely convicted or accused. Some of these kits have been sitting around for years. The worst part of this travesty is that federal money had been given to law enforcement agencies to process the rape kits. They decided to use the money for something else. This is the grossest demeaning of the courage that it took for these women to come forward.

Women: you have half the votes! You should be kicking ass and taking names. Let's look at some more facts:

- Women make seventy-seven percent of what men make for doing the same job. As a result, many single mothers and their children live in poverty.

- Four women per day are murdered by a domestic partner.

- There are many in government who are openly and

relentlessly trying to take away a woman's choice concerning her reproductive rights.

Earlier, I said that equal rights for women were the last frontier of the civil rights movement. Actually, that statement is inadequate to describe the gross mistreatment of women in our county. Rape and the killing of women are beyond discrimination. These are our most serious crimes, occurring with unbelievable frequency. Rape in our military is rape within the United States government itself. I daresay that on the whole, women are treated worse than any other group in our country. For every American—regardless of gender, race, politics, or anything else—this should be absolutely unacceptable. It must be stopped.

The discrimination against and mistreatment of women has been going on for so long and is so pervasive that even some women seem complacent about it. One of the main components—if not *the* main component of discrimination and repression—is, again, the "big lie." Bigots and tyrants throughout history have used it in an attempt to control people and "keep them in their place." The idea is that if you tell people over and over again that they are inferior, soon they will start to believe it.

This is obviously not unique to women. Slave-owners' message to African Americans was that we were absolutely inferior to white people, in every facet of life. One effect was that light-skinned African Americans looked down on dark-skinned African Americans. My best friend in grade school, for instance, was teased so mercilessly for the darkness of his skin that at one point he started using some kind of facial cream to lighten it. A black-owned beauty products company made the product. Some black people, men and women, used chemical-laden hair products to straighten their hair, so that it resembled white people's hair. A few all-black colleges would not admit applicants if their skin was too dark. When I was growing up, my mother and I knew an African American gentleman who owned and ran a successful grocery store. When he was looking to hire a butcher, the employment agency sent him a butcher who was white. After a while, we noticed that the butcher was no longer working there. When my mother asked the owner what had happened, the owner said, "It's just not right for a white man to work for a black man."

Now I understand and appreciate more than ever what my mother constantly impressed upon me: that in the deepest sense, I was no better than anybody, and that nobody was better than me. My generation's refrain to reject all of the "big lies" was this: "Say it loud: I'm black and I'm proud!" This is the fundamental message that we should bestow upon all of our children, regardless of gender. Be proud of who you are. It is the message inherent in the United States Constitution to all of us.

My personal experience with the "big lie" of sexism came to me through my daughter. She had just started first grade. One day when she came home after school, I told her that there was a program on television about being an astronaut that we could watch together. I told her maybe she'd want to be an astronaut someday. She looked at me and said, "Daddy, that's boys' stuff." I was stunned. Inside, I was angry. I remember saying to myself that "they" have gotten to her already. She is only a first grader, and our society is trying to impose limitations on her ambitions. As her father, I knew I had to be as vigilant with her as my mother was with me, keeping the "big lies" out of her thinking, and constantly reminding her that there are no limits, and she can be whatever she wants to be.

While women must lead the way in claiming their equality, every American should stand up against injustice, as so many did for the black and other civil rights movements. For example, I personally believe that most of the sexual assaults in our military and on our campuses are being committed by a relatively small number of serial sexual predators. They will be rooted out and punished only when men and women soldiers and students stand up and report them, demanding justice. Will you stand up for freedom, fairness, and opportunity for all? Are you a Great American?

RESTORE VOTING RIGHTS ACT

In 1965, when television broadcast the ugly and brutal beating of participants in a peaceful march for voting rights that occurred in Selma, Alabama, the public was shocked. We were appalled at the violence police unleashed on these peaceful protesters, who were attacked with nightsticks, whips, and tear gas. After decades of voter suppression for minorities following the Fifteenth Amendment (passed in 1870, this amendment prohibited states from denying a male citizen the right to vote based on "race, color or previous condition of servitude"), citizens stood up and marched to stop the continuing suppression of voting rights for African Americans in the Southern states. They were met with unrelenting violence.

Following the violence and outrage, President Lyndon Johnson called for comprehensive voting rights laws to stop the suppression of discrimination at the polls, after laying out the numerous ways in which election officials denied African American citizens to vote. The Voting Rights Act was passed shortly after, ensuring that state and local governments did not pass laws that restricted American citizens from the equal right to vote based on race.

In 2013, The United States Supreme Court ruled that Section 4 of this landmark Voting Rights Act, which required certain parts of the country with a history of racial discrimination to clear changes to their voting laws with the Federal Government, was invalid.

It's not just blacks that need this protection. It's everybody who won't vote the way "they" want. It's not based on race anymore. Officials have been purging voter rolls, hoping people will be so frustrated that they won't vote. Often, the ones most affected are the poor and elderly. The idea that an elected official would try to keep people from voting is absurd. We have fought too long and too hard to hand our country over to these elitists.

The fight dates back to the 1800s, when women had few legal rights and were not allowed to vote. It is epitomized by the speech Susan B. Anthony gave after her arrest for casting a ballot in the 1872 Presidential election. According to *History Place*, "She was tried and then fined $100, but refused to pay":[35]

> Friends and fellow citizens: I stand before you tonight under indictment for the alleged crime of having voted at the last presidential election, without having a lawful right to vote. It shall be my work this evening to prove to you that in thus voting, I not only committed no crime, but, instead, simply exercised my citizen's rights, guaranteed to me and all United States citizens by the National Constitution, beyond the power of any state to deny.
>
> The preamble of the Federal Constitution says:
>
> > "We, the people of the United States, in order to form a more perfect union, establish justice, insure domestic tranquility, provide for the common defense, promote the general welfare, and secure the blessings of liberty to ourselves and our posterity, do ordain and establish this Constitution for the United States of America."
>
> It was we, the people; not we, the white male citizens; nor yet we, the male citizens; but we, the whole people, who formed the Union. And we formed it, not to give the blessings of liberty, but to secure them; not

to the half of ourselves and the half of our posterity, but to the whole people - women as well as men. And it is a downright mockery to talk to women of their enjoyment of the blessings of liberty while they are denied the use of the only means of securing them provided by this democratic-republican government - the ballot.

For any state to make sex a qualification that must ever result in the disfranchisement of one entire half of the people, is to pass a bill of attainder, or, an ex post facto law, and is therefore a violation of the supreme law of the land. By it the blessings of liberty are forever withheld from women and their female posterity.

To them this government has no just powers derived from the consent of the governed. To them this government is not a democracy. It is not a republic. It is an odious aristocracy; a hateful oligarchy of sex; the most hateful aristocracy ever established on the face of the globe; an oligarchy of wealth, where the rich govern the poor. An oligarchy of learning, where the educated govern the ignorant, or even an oligarchy of race, where the Saxon rules the African, might be endured; but this oligarchy of sex, which makes father, brothers, husband, sons, the oligarchs over the mother and sisters, the wife and daughters, of every household - which ordains all men sovereigns, all women subjects, carries dissension, discord, and rebellion into every home of the nation.

Webster, Worcester, and Bouvier all define a citizen to be a person in the United States, entitled to vote and hold office.

The only question left to be settled now is: Are women persons? And I hardly believe any of our opponents will have the hardihood to say they are not. Being persons, then, women are citizens; and no state has a right to make any law, or to enforce any old law, that shall abridge their privileges or immunities. Hence, every discrimination against women in the constitutions and laws of the several states is today null and void, precisely as is every one against Negroes.

Susan B. Anthony - 1873[36]

The struggle for the right to vote in America was hard fought. Yet in the last few years we have a proliferation of restrictions being put into place to deter voting. Journalist Ari Berman, in his new book *Give Us the Ballot,* reports that from 2011 to 2015, forty-nine states introduced 395 new voting restrictions.[37] *The New York Times* reported June 5, 2015 that more than 50 million Americans are not registered to vote.[38] Given that only thirty-six percent of eligible voters voted in the last election, we should be doing everything, and I mean everything, to encourage voting in America. Underserved people need to vote. No one will pay any attention until you do. Take back your power and vote!

CONCLUSION

IN THE END, BEING A GREAT AMERICAN IS ABOUT STANDING UP FOR the American Dream. The purpose of our government is to serve us by giving each American an opportunity to make a better life for themselves. The middle-class American, and those who aspire to the middle class, embody what the American Dream is all about. It is having a genuine shot at making a better life for ourselves.

This is not about taking from the rich and giving to the poor. It's not about handouts. It is about investment in human capital, our country's most important and valuable resource—its people, all of them—and the best investment that can be made with our tax dollars. It is about striving for our biggest dreams, with a real chance of making them come true—whether that means becoming super-rich, a concert violinist, or someone who spends a lot of time fishing. It is about knowing that our children and grandchildren will have an opportunity for a better life than their parents. For the first time in our history, our children are expected to be worse off than we are, both economically and in terms of their health. What does this say about our values as a people, if we won't even vote for the sake of our children?

The American Dream is not just about us, it is vital to the greatness of our country. The more the quality of life improves for the American people, the stronger and wealthier our country becomes. Previous generations of Americans worked, fought, and died so we could be free and have it better than before. Now, some super-rich elitists who believe that the American Dream is only for them and their children have bought our government. Are we going to lie down and let them take it away from us? Our elected officials, especially in the Congress, have sold us out for campaign money and because they know that we don't care enough to hold them accountable with our votes. They have no respect for us, because we don't vote. They have no fear of us, because we don't vote.

And why should they respect us if we won't stand up for ourselves with our votes? Why should they respect us when we won't even stand up for our children with our votes? Why should they respect us when they know that we have all of the power with our votes, and still line up like sheep to be used up and cast aside?

The only thing that is more powerful than their money is our vote—and they know it. That is why they are working so hard and spending so much to take our right to vote away from us. They fear the power of our votes. If we don't strike that fear into them, they will continue to grind the American middle class down until the American Dream is nothing more than a cruel hoax. It is on us.

THE GOLD STANDARD FOR BEING A GREAT AMERICAN!

The gold standard for being a great American comes from the

[handwritten marginalia: UNION MEMBERS, PRO-LABOR, VALUES OF LIBERAL, WOMEN'S CHOICE, EQUAL RIGHTS; LOW LIFE LOB OR, DON'T SUPPORT POLITICIANS BECAUSE, GUN CONTROL, LIKE]

LGBT community and the NRA. While these two groups may be far apart on the political spectrum, and you may approve or disapprove of what they stand for, they are the supreme examples of being a Great American, because they vote! They are feared by politicians because they vote! They got what they wanted from politicians because they vote! They care about themselves and their issues enough to get up off their butts and vote. They know which politicians are working for them, and which are working against them, and they vote accordingly. They hold their representatives accountable. They understand how politicians think. To politicians, if you don't vote, then you don't count. To politicians, if you don't vote, then you are a nobody. These Great Americans also understand that if they vote and the rest of us don't, then they have all of the power, because they get all of the attention of the politicians.

The reason that the American middle class is shrinking into poverty is because politicians ignore or even hurt us because we don't vote. They have no fear of us because we don't vote. They know we don't care enough to watch them and hold them accountable! Politicians know that we can be easily manipulated if they spend huge amounts of money on propaganda, spreading the message of the super-rich and powerful people they really work for.

Each of us has the power to be a Great American, because we are blessed to live in the US, where our vote really counts. Remember, the 2000 Presidential election was decided by 537 votes out of 6,000,000 votes cast in Florida. As I said earlier, in 1980 I lost my race for the Oregon House of Representatives by sixty-one votes. Are we going to use our power like the LGBT community and the NRA to better ourselves and the country, or are we going to continue to be suckers, chumps, and nobodies?

We must elect people to office who will invest in our education, training, and small businesses. Then this magnificent nation will prosper beyond imagination, as intended by the American Dream. Please be a Great American and VOTE. Our Country needs you!

Thank you for taking the time to read this.

Jim Hill

ENDNOTES

1   *Mother Jones* promotion (undated).

2   *Americans for Tax Fairness,* "Corporate Tax Dodgers," 2013
    Report, page 9, http://www.americansfortaxfairness.org/files/
    Corporate-Tax-Dodgers-Report-Final.pdf

3   George Orwell (Eric Blair), *Animal Farm: A Fairy Story.* New
    York: Houghton Mifflin Harcourt, 1987.

4   US Department of Treasury 2012 report

5   Mamta Badkar, "The Number Of US Homes Lost To
    Foreclosures Plunged 27%," Business Insider, July 9, 2013,
    "National Foreclosure Report" December 2013, http://www.
    businessinsider.com/completed-us-foreclosures-fall-27-2013-7

6   "The Financial Crisis Response" In Charts April 2012
    www.treasury.gov/resource-center/data-chart-center/
    documents/20120413_FinancialCrisisResponse.pdf

7   Rachel Beck and Matthew Fordahl, "AP IMPACT: CEO pay
    chugs up in '07 despite economy," *USA Today,* June 16, 2008,
    http://usatoday30.usatoday.com/money/economy/2008-06-16-
    354405217_x.htm

8   Michael Grunwald, "The Real Silver Lining of the Absurd AIG Lawsuit," *Time*, October 6, 2014, http://time.com/3475826/aig-lawsuit-geithner-bernanke-greenberg/

9   Aaron M. Kessler , "Ex-A.I.G. Chief wins Bailout suit, but Gets No Damages," *New York Times*, June 15, 2015, http://www.nytimes.com/2015/06/16/business/dealbook/judge-sides-with-ex-aig-chief-greenberg-against-us-but-awards-no-money.html?_r=0

10 Michael Boyle, "How the US public was defrauded by the hidden cost of the Iraq War," *Guardian*, March 11, 2013, http://www.theguardian.com/commentisfree/2013/mar/11/us-public-defrauded-hidden-cost-iraq-war

11 Campaign for America's Future, "Ten Years of the Bush Tax Cuts Benefiting the Rich," https://ourfuture.org/fact_sheet/ten-years-bush-tax-cuts-benefiting-rich

12 George Orwell, *Nineteen Eighty-Four*; New York: New American Library, 2003, page 147

13 Dan Alexander, "Super Donor Sheldon Adelson Made $2.1 Billion in 2 Days Since 'Adelson Primary,'" *Forbes*, April 2, 2014, http://onforb.es/1i2tXFq

14 Michael Grunwald, "The Party of No: New Details on the GOP Plot to Obstruct Obama," *Time*, August 23, 2012, http://swampland.time.com/2012/08/23/the-party-of-no-new-details-on-the-gop-plot-to-obstruct-obama/.

15 The Center for Media and Democracy hosts website: Source Watch http://www.sourcewatch.org/index.php/tea-party

16 Jane Mayer, "Covert Operations: The billionaire brothers who are waging a war against Obama," *The New Yorker*, August 30, 2010, http://www.newyorker.com/magazine/2010/08/30/covert-operations

17 Kirby Dick, *The Invisible War*, directed by Kirby Dick, Chain Camera Pictures, 2012

18 Gina Kolata, "Death Rates Rising for Middle-Aged White

Americans, Study Finds," *New York Times*, November 2, 2015, http://www.nytimes.com/2015/11/03/health/death-rates-rising-for-middle-aged-white-americans-study-finds.html

19 David Woolner, "How FDR Took on the Forces of Wealth and Power," *Roosevelt Institute*, November 25, 2009, http://rooseveltinstitute.org/how-fdr-took-forces-wealth-and-power/

20 Tim Dickinson, *Rolling Stone*; "Inside the Koch Brothers' Toxic Empire," September 24, 2014, http://www.rollingstone.com/politics/news/inside-the-koch-brothers-toxic-empire-20140924

21 *Democracy Now!*, "The Kochs' Anti-Civil Rights Roots: New Docs Expose Charles Koch's Ties to John Birch Society," July 8, 2014, http://www.democracynow.org/2014/7/8/kochs_anti_civil_rights_roots

22 Trymaine Lee, "The Koch Brothers and The Battle Over Integration In Wake County's Schools," *Huffington Post*, August 15, 2011. See also Robert Greenwald, *Koch Brothers Exposed*, Bravenewfilms.org

23 Frank Rich, "The Billionaires Bankrolling the Tea Party," *New York Times*, August 28, 2010, http://www.nytimes.com/2010/08/29/opinion/29rich.html

24 Edward Bernays quoted by Michael Pirsch, "Class Warfare, the Final Chapter," *Truthout*, March 15, 2011, http://truth-out.org/archive/component/k2/item/94744:class-warfare-the-final-chapter

25 Ann Kennings, *Maya Angelou: In Her Words*, Raleigh, North Carolina: Lulu Press, 2014.

26 Alfred Lord Tennyson, "The Charge of the Light Brigade," *Poetry Foundation*, http://poetryfoundation.org/poem/174586

27 *New York Times*, "Let the People Vote" (editorial), 06-05-15.

28 Susan Page, "McConnell: Unyielding on Iran, defiant on Koch brothers," *USA Today*, April 1, 2015, http://usatoday.com/story/news/politics/2015/01/28/capital-download-mitch-mcconnell-interview-obama/22468577

29 Mayday.us/the-plan/

30 Fair Politics (http://fairpoliticsus.org/) reports on Mayday.us proposals. In particular, see: "The Conversation at Hand," http://fairpoliticsus.org/the-solution/.

31 For more, see the following links: American Anti-Corruption Act (http://anticorruptionact.org/full-text/); Empowering Citizens Act (http://www.democracy21.org/ppf-notes/press-releases-ppf-notes/a-summary-of-h-r-6448-the-empowering-citizens-act-2/); Government By the People Act (https://sarbanes.house.gov/bythepeople); Political Money Reform Proposal (http://jimrubens.com/issues/agenda); Taxation Only With Representation Act (http://legalethicsforum.typepad.com/blog/2014/03/federal-and-state-constitutional-amendments-and-statutes-providing-for-taxation-only-with-representa.html)

32 Ralph Benko, "Lawrence Lessig Shows That Today's Political Struggle Has Nothing To Do With Democrats Vs. Republicans," *Forbes*, November 24, 2014, http://forbes.com/sites/ralphbenko/2014/11/24/Lawrence-lessig-shows-that-todays-political-struggle-has-nothing-to-do-with-democrats-vs-republicans

33 Emma Lazarus, "The New Colossus," *Poetry Foundation*, http://www.poetryfoundation.org/poem/175887

34 Steve Reilly, "Tens of thousands of rape kits go untested across USA," *USA Today*, July 17, 2015, http://www.usatoday.com/story/news/2015/07/16/untested-rape-kits-evidence-across-usa/29902199/

35 *History Place*, http://historyplace.com/speeches/Anthony.htm

36 Susan B. Anthony, "On Women's Right to Vote," *History Place*, historyplace.com/speeches/anthony.htm

37 Ari Berman, *Give Us the Ballot*, New York: Farrar, Straus and Giroux, 2015.

38 *New York Times*, "Let the People Vote" (editorial), 06-05-15.

JIM HILL

WAS BORN IN Atlanta, Georgia, in 1947, and raised there by his single mother. After growing up in the segregated South, he received a BA in economics from Michigan State University in 1969, an MBA from Indiana University in 1971, and a JD from Indiana University College of Law in 1974.

Jim moved to Salem, Oregon, in 1974, where he raised a bi-racial daughter, Jennifer, and worked as an Assistant Attorney General at the Oregon Department of Justice. He went on to become an Oregon State Representative in 1983 and an Oregon State Senator in 1987. Some of his accomplishments were co-sponsoring the establishment of a holiday in honor of Martin Luther King, Jr., passing the Anti-Apartheid

Act, creating the Oregon Resource and Technology Development Corporation (supplying seed capital to Oregon businesses), and introducing the bill to allow Oregon State Lottery funds to enhance Oregon's economy.

Jim became the first person of color to be elected to a state-wide office in Oregon, serving two terms as State Treasurer beginning in 1993. During his tenure in this position, he oversaw an improvement of the state's bond rating, and the creation of the Oregon Growth Account—an investment program exclusively dedicated to providing seed and venture capital dollars to Oregon businesses. Jim worked to improve financial literacy, and held the "Every Woman's Money Conference" to provide women with the tools they needed to succeed financially. He then ran unsuccessfully for Governor of the State of Oregon.

Jim has served on several important boards: the Northwest Health Foundation, the Oregon Assembly for Black Affairs, the Oregon National Bar Association, NARAL, and the National Association of State Treasurers—where he served as President.

Jim lives in Salem, Oregon, where he remains committed to making a difference through the power of the written word.

MYTH SUPPORTING EDUCATION:
THOSE WHO HAVE THE BEST EDUCATION + TRAINING
GET THE HIGHEST PAY FOR THEIR INFORMED DECISIONS
ie GOOD DECISIONS ABOUT VERY EXPENSIVE PROJECTS
SHOULD BE 'REWARDED' IN PROPORTION.
∴ SMART PEOPLE CONTRIBUTE HIGH VALUE,
GET PAID A LOT, GET TAXED A LOT TOO,
+ WE CAN HAVE LESS GOV'T DEBT.

p65 ¿ 70% OF OUR ECONOMY IS MIDDLE CLASS CONSUMER

p69 VAGRANCY LAWS — DO THEY STILL DO THIS TO
PROVIDE CHEAP SLAVE LABOR?
WERE THEY JUST FOR BLACKS?

p73 WHEN DID COMPANIES STOP USING PRIVATE MILITIAS?

p88 WHAT DO PROPOSALS FOR CAMPAIGN FINANCE
REFORM LOOK LIKE? WHO IS LEADING?
THIS?

p93 CHECK OUT WHAT GEORGE VOINOVICH IS WRIT-
ING ABOUT THESE DAYS (AN EX-SENATOR?)

p102 IS OIL IN IRAN THE REASON WHY GOP IS OPPOSED
TO THE IRAN NUCLEAR LIMITATION DEAL?

p103 WHO IS IN THE TEA PARTY CAUCUS
WHO SIGNED THE IRAN LETTER DISSING THE
IRAN DEAL?

p106 HOW MUCH DO WE GIVE TO ISRAEL?
IS IT STILL CLOSE TO $3B/YR?

p108 WHAT IS BOEHNER UP TO? IS HE WORKING FOR
ISRAEL YET?

PLUTOCRATS — POWERED BY WEALTH

LEARN TO 'DIG IN'
'GET THE DIRT'
ie HAVE FACTS w/ WHICH TO
ARGUE — SO THAT I'M NOT
BRAINWASHED BY PLATITUDES
& STRONG OPINIONS

KOCH BROTHERS
MURDOCH

CPSIA information can be obtained
at www.ICGtesting.com
Printed in the USA
FSOW01n1923030916
24571FS

9 781629 013503